Praise for *Robert E. Lee on Leadership*

"*Robert E. Lee on Leadership* is not only the best brief biography of Lee that I have found, but the presentation of leadership principles extracted from and organized around the various periods of Lee's life is superior even to the popular books by Stephen R. Covey."
> —BRYANT BURROUGHS, associate editor,
> *The Southern Partisan*

"In very readable prose, Crocker . . . reviews Lee's career not only in the military but as a farmer and college president. . . . Thought-provoking ideas for today's present and future leaders."
> —*Library Journal*

"Harry Crocker has provided a great service by reminding us through this moving and tightly written biography that winning isn't the only thing: faithfulness and honor live in our memories after the guns are silent."
> —MARVIN OLASKY, author of the bestselling
> *Renewing American Compassion* and
> *The American Leadership Tradition*

"It appears to be a sacrosanct duty of leftist college professors . . . to destroy American heroes, one brave soul at a time. That won't happen to Robert E. Lee—not if H. W. Crocker III has anything to say about it. And he does. In fact, Crocker's *Robert E. Lee on Leadership* not only stands boldly athwart the revisionist bent of the radical historicists; it also locates nuggets of wisdom on the leadership style of America's greatest military genius."
> —*Campus*

"There is much to be gained by reading this book, which is like bolting down a glass of cold water on a hot day."
> —*Human Events*

"Crocker captures the essential Lee."
> —DOUG BANDOW, *The Washington Times*

"*Robert E. Lee on Leadership* gives us more than an account of battles, it gives us an accurate and sensitive portrait of the heart of Lee."
> —*One Sword at Least*

ROBERT E. LEE ON LEADERSHIP

Executive Lessons in Character, Courage, and Vision

H . W . C R O C K E R   I I I

THREE RIVERS PRESS

NEW YORK

To Sally and the boys

Published by Three Rivers Press, New York, New York.
Member of the Crown Publishing Group, a division of Random House, Inc.
www.crownpublishing.com

THREE RIVERS PRESS and the Tugboat design are registered trademarks of Random House, Inc.

Originally published by Prima Publishing, Roseville, California, in 2000.

Printed in the United States of America

Library of Congress Cataloging-in-Publication Data
Crocker, H. W.
Robert E. Lee on leadership : executive lessons in character, courage, and vision / H. W. Crocker, III.
p.   cm.
Includes bibliographical references and index.
1. Lee, Robert E. (Robert Edward), 1807–1870—Military leadership.
2. Generals—Confederate States of America Biography. 3. Command of troops.
4. Leadership Case studies. 5. Management—United States Case studies. I. Title.
E467.1.L4C8 1999
973.7'3'092—dc21   99-15074

ISBN 0-7615-2554-8
ISBN-13 978-0-7615-2554-7

10 9 8 7

First Edition

But leadership is only courage and wisdom,
and a great carelessness of self.

—JOHN BUCHAN, *A Prince of the Captivity*

CONTENTS

THE GREY FOX

THEY CALLED HIM "the Grey Fox," and with good reason. Packs of blue-coated hounds, led now by General Ulysses S. Grant, had tried for three years to run him to ground, and failed. Every time he seemed cornered, he fooled his pursuers, snapped at their heels, and sent them scurrying away. Now shells were exploding around him. His steady, dapple-grey horse, Traveller, exhibiting a sort of sixth sense, reared as shot plunged through the smoke of battle, passing under his belly, sparking beneath the spurs of General Robert E. Lee. Lee's brown eyes glinted; the Grey Fox was going to strike again. Outnumbered as always, nearly two to one, his lines dissolving under an assault by the better-fed, better-clothed, better-equipped Union foe, Lee turned Traveller toward the enemy. With gauntleted hand, he brushed dirt from the broad chest of his grey uniform. His jaw clenched. He would counterattack.

"Go back, General Lee! For God's sake, go back!" the men shouted, as they had done at the Wilderness, and as they had done again only the day before, as their beloved general rode to the front, unarmed but apparently preparing to charge the Federals—"those people"—and push them back himself.

"If you promise to drive those people from our works, I will go back," Lee replied.

The men rushed forward, yelling their promise, and slammed into their former entrenchments, driving the Federals out of them. The battle raged all day at the "Bloody Angle" to the north of Spotsylvania Court House, until nearly 10,000 Confederates and 18,000 Federals were lost as casualties. Even the relentless Grant, who was willing "to fight it out on this line if it takes all summer"—which it would, and longer—and who was willing to suffer any number of losses in ceaseless pursuit of Lee, waited nine days for 30,000 fresh reinforcements before renewing his attack, numbers that weren't available to Lee.

Grant's reinforcements, however, wouldn't be enough. The Grey Fox was still too clever, still packed too much of a bite, however tattered, hungry, and desperate his forces appeared.

"We must strike them a blow," said Lee. And they did, stinging blows that cost Grant nearly 1,700 casualties a day— at least 50,000 men in the single month of May 1864. While victory for the South seemed increasingly impossible—with Atlanta besieged and the North's massive superiority in industry and manpower weighing heavily—defeating Lee seemed equally impossible, unless he and his Army of Northern Virginia could be ground into dust in a pounding war of attrition that counted no costs, that was willing to lose two men to every one of Lee's, and that would continue until every last remnant of Lee's gallant army was starved, weaponless, or dead.

In fact, the war would last for eleven more months; its close at Appomattox Court House was one of the most poignant moments in American history, with Lee's "General Orders No. 9," his farewell to the Army of Northern Virginia, becoming the funeral ode for "the Lost Cause," the Gettysburg Address of the South:

After four years of arduous service, marked by unsurpassed courage and fortitude, the Army of Northern Virginia has been compelled to yield to overwhelming numbers and resources.

I need not tell the brave survivors of so many hard-fought battles, who have remained steadfast to the last, that I have consented to the result from no distrust of them.

But, feeling that valor and devotion could accomplish nothing that could compensate for the loss that must have attended the continuance of the contest, I determined to avoid the useless sacrifice of those whose past services have endeared them to their countrymen.

By the terms of the agreement officers and men can return to their homes and remain until exchanged. You will take with you the satisfaction that proceeds from the consciousness of duty faithfully performed; and I earnestly pray that a merciful God will extend to you his blessing and protection.

With an increasing admiration of your constancy and devotion to your country, and a grateful remembrance of your kind and generous considerations for myself, I bid you all an affectionate farewell.

One should never underestimate what the War Between the States cost Robert E. Lee. A successful soldier, he was not used to defeat. Now he had lost his home, his career, and virtually all his worldly goods—including his carefully harbored savings and investments. Worse, he had suffered the premature death of a daughter, a daughter-in-law, two grandchildren, and countless colleagues and friends. A patriot who had devoted his life to the service of his country, who venerated George Washington, who was the son of a Revolutionary War hero ("Light Horse Harry" Lee), and who had married Martha Washington's great-granddaughter, was now deprived of his citizenship and liable to be tried for treason. His home state of Virginia was under occupation, its citizens deprived of their rights, its fields, towns, and cities devastated by the Union's policy of total war.

And yet . . . and yet, Lee was *not* defeated. Soon after the war's end, he was increasingly regarded not merely as a military genius but as someone to be venerated by the South *and* by the North, to be venerated, indeed, throughout the Western world as a great man.

As Winston Churchill would later write, Lee was "one of the noblest Americans who ever lived, and one of the greatest captains known to the annals of war."

Another Englishman, Lee's contemporary, Field Marshall Viscount Wolseley, wrote of him: "I desire to make known to the reader not only the renowned soldier, whom I believe to have been the greatest of his age, but to give some insight into the character of one whom I have always considered the most perfect man I ever met. . . . I have met many of the great men of my time, but Lee alone impressed me with the feeling that I was in the presence of a man who was cast in a grander mould, and made of different and of finer metal than all other men."

President Theodore Roosevelt, scion of a Yankee father and a Southern mother, thought Lee was "without any exception the very greatest of all the great captains that the English-speaking peoples have brought forth."

In our own time, the New Jersey–born Pulitzer Prize–winning novelist, Michael Shaara, author of *The Killer Angels,* called Lee "perhaps the most beloved General in the history of American war."

One of the most popular contemporary Civil War historians, the Pulitzer Prize–winning James McPherson of Princeton University, author of the best-selling *Battle Cry of Freedom,* has called Lee the "greatest tactician and most charismatic commander" of the Civil War, and a "'gentleman' in the classic sense of that word and a worthy representation of the Virginia gentry that did so much to shape the early history of the United States."

In the American South, of course, Lee became an icon, a Christlike figure of unblemished character, who rejected temptation (when he was offered command of the Union armies at the start of the war), who suffered, and who eventually gave himself up to redeem his countrymen by his example of fortitude, forgiveness, and reconciliation. He was a paragon, and a defense. If the South could produce such a man, how could the North consider Southern civilization benighted?

Lee was bred, trained, and conducted himself as a leader of men—one of the most successful leaders in American history. He shaped the most effective fighting force on the American continent, a force that even after four grueling years of combat, after the men's bellies were ironed to their backbones by lack of provisions, after their hopes of independence were cut to the dirt they stood on, still greeted Lee as he returned from his historic meeting with Grant by shouting: "General! General! Are we surrendered? General, say the word. Say the word, General, and we'll go after them again!"

Leadership was defined by James McGregor Burns as "leaders acting—as well as caring, inspiring and persuading others to act—for certain shared goals that represent the values—the wants and needs, the aspirations and expectations—of themselves and the people they represent." It is a role that virtually all of us are called to play—if not as great generals, then as parents, as members of our communities, or as supervisors or managers at work.

This book attempts to highlight Lee's principles and, more important, Lee's examples of leadership. It does not, as many such books do, artificially apportion anecdotes from a life to support management clichés. If, as the poet Alexander Pope said, "the proper study of mankind is man," then it is important to *know the man,* to get the full life, to understand the parameters within which he operated and the drama in which he played a part, to see his life with its beginning, its middle, and its end, though with the emphasis on what is the focus of this book: Lee's leadership in war and peace, with the most salient points bulleted at the end of each chapter.

This is a book for the businessman—the vocation that most Americans are called to perform—seeking guidance on how to lead a business, employees, subordinates. But it is also a book for the *whole* man, because, as one of Lee's most perceptive biographers, Emory Thomas, has noted: "Lee was a great person, not so much because of what he did (although his accomplishments were extraordinary); he was great because of the way he lived, because of what he was." Lee's lessons of leadership go beyond managing people nine to five and beyond the leadership of men wreathed in the smoke of battle, though the former is our point and the latter our method of illumination. Lee's lessons offer a *way to live.*

Though a professional soldier, Lee always dreamed of being a small businessman, an independent farmer. As an educator, he sought to train his students in practical skills that would rebuild the economy of the postwar South. But while he put enormous value on the benefits of commerce and financial independence, he would also have agreed with German free-market economist Wilhelm Röpke (who, like Lee, helped restore a shattered civilization) that "the vital things are those beyond supply and demand and the world of property. It is they which give meaning, dignity, and inner richness to life, those purposes and values which belong to the realm of ethics in the widest sense."

In our own materialistic age, we can especially benefit from Lee's example of leadership, which reminds us that ultimately what matters is not how much money we have made, how many businesses we have led or acquired, how many jobs we have created, or how many "toys" we have accumulated, but who we are.

And Lee is an ever-present reminder that we can be much more.

CHAPTER ONE

UNDERSTANDING LEE

LEE WAS BORN an aristocrat. His family, on his father's side, had been in Virginia since 1641. His lineage could be traced back to the Norman Conquest and to knights who rode with William the Conqueror and Richard the Lion-hearted. Of the Lees of Virginia, future president John Adams wrote: "The family of Lee . . . has more men of merit in it than any other family."

Lee's mother, Ann Hill Carter, was, if anything, even more blue-blooded. The Carters had been in Virginia since the beginning of the 17th century, and her father, Charles "King" Carter, was the largest landholder in the state. King Carter frankly doubted that Lee's father, "Light Horse Harry" Lee, was good enough for his daughter.

His doubts had some foundation. For if Robert E. Lee was born to privilege, he was also born to trouble. Light Horse Harry, although a successful cavalry officer and a favorite of General George Washington, could be impetuous in carrying out orders. Once during their service together in the Revolutionary War, Light Horse Harry received Washington's permission to enforce swift justice on deserters. The enterprising cavalryman promptly found a deserter, had him hanged, and then had his head lopped off and delivered, still bleeding, to the future first president of the United States.

But swashbuckling Harry was not suited to civilian life. By the time he courted Ann Hill Carter, he was fast gaining a reputation as a ne'er-do-well. Over the course of his colorful life—during which he served as Virginia's governor and volunteered to serve as a mercenary officer in the French Revolution (marriage to Ann Hill Carter stayed him)—he succeeded only in impoverishing his family by selling tracts of his inherited land to support various financial schemes that inevitably failed. He was even jailed as a debtor.

But worse was to come. In 1812, Light Horse Harry visited a friend in Baltimore who published a newspaper opposed to America's new war with Britain. The newspaper's offices were besieged by a mob of "patriots." Light Horse Harry, trapped in the building with his friend, bravely mounted a defense. The Maryland militia intervened, taking the newspaper publisher, Light Horse Harry, and the others who had been locked in the building into the protective custody of the local jail. The mob, however, broke into the jail, beat one of the "protected" men to death and pummeled eight others so severely that they were left for dead. Light Horse Harry was among that battered number, and he never fully recovered. In the summer of 1813, the Revolutionary War hero exiled himself to the West Indies to recuperate and attempt to restore his shattered finances. His son Robert was six years old. Robert E. Lee never saw his father again. In 1818, his life's flame flickering, Light Horse Harry Lee sailed for Virginia, but had to put ashore on Cumberland Island, Georgia, where he died and was buried.

The Lee family scandals didn't die with him, however. Henry Lee IV, Light Horse Harry's son by a previous marriage, so stained the family name that he earned the moniker "Black

Horse Harry" Lee. His wife became a morphine addict after their two-year-old daughter died after falling off the steps of their house. Her frustrated and alienated husband then committed adultery with her sister, who was his ward, and accumulated debts that forced the sale of Stratford, the stately home where Robert E. Lee was born.

While these scandals touched Robert E. Lee materially—he was raised, in modern parlance, by a "single" mother who, though born to vast estates, had little personal wealth and no land of her own—in other ways, the scandals barely touched him at all. He and his father hardly knew each other. Light Horse Harry mentioned his younger son in a letter only once, saying that he was "always good . . . [with a] happy turn of mind." The misadventures of Lee's distant and much older half brother were also largely irrelevant to him, except, of course, as they might have become, however softened, cautionary tales from his mother.

For Robert E. Lee's mother was compelled to practice prudence, and certainly had every desire for her young son to avoid the waywardness of his father and half brother. It would be easy to imagine that these object lessons of family failures and misdeeds would have left lasting scars on the boy, but in Robert E. Lee's case, growing up under the emollient, latitudinarian Anglican tradition of the Virginia aristocracy, this never happened. Lee was not only a bright, happy, helpful, conscientious, muscular boy, he was, from the start, an exemplar of the best aristocratic traditions that had been bred into him.

If he was forced into an early maturity, it only added to the luster of his character; it did not compromise his sense of humor or degenerate into priggishness. Even as a young man, he was noted for his poise, his charm, his dutifulness, his bearing. As a young cadet at West Point, he was already touted as "the marble model"—not because he was cold, but because he was *perfect:* the handsomest man in his class, with a graceful, athletic body, built on an expansive chest that tapered like an inverted pyramid down to miniature (size four-and-a-half) feet. He graduated without a single demerit on his record, second in his class academically, and was noted for his dignified but easy manner. He was the very personification of the gentlemanly ideal and *of a leader*—the sort of man others instinctively looked to for guidance and naturally followed.

It is true that Robert E. Lee was a product of his time, his genetics, and the traditions of an Attic Virginia that was the cradle of Periclean Americans like Thomas Jefferson, George Washington, James Madison, James Monroe, Patrick Henry, George Mason, and John Marshall (whose grandson would become one of Lee's closest wartime aides), among many others.

It was a Virginia remembered by Edward Eggleston in his *Rebel's Recollections:*

> It was a very beautiful and enjoyable life that the Virginians led in that ancient time, for it certainly seems ages ago, before the war came to turn ideas upside down and convert the picturesque commonwealth into a commonplace, modern state. It was a soft, dreamy, deliciously quiet life, a life of repose, an old life, with all its sharp corners and rough surfaces long ago worn round and smooth. Everything fitted everything else, and every point in it was as well settled as to leave no work of improvement for anybody to do. The Virginians were satisfied with things as they were, and if there were reformers born among them, they went elsewhere to work their changes. Society in the Old Dominion was like a well-rolled and closely packed gravel walk, in which each pebble has found precisely the place it fits best. There was no giving way under one's feet, no uncomfortable grinding of loose materials as one walked about over the firm and long-used ways of the Virginia social life.

It was a time, confessedly, much different from our own cybertech age, where such an Old South vision of a slow-moving, ordered, profoundly conservative and aristocratic society might be scorned by some as stuffy, repressive, and unproductive, or, at best, as a hopeless reactionary dream that can never be recreated—or, with the then-existence of slavery, *should* never be recovered. In any event, today our hopes for producing men like America's Virginia-born Founding Fathers are about as distant as our hopes of hearing news of rising SAT scores, the growing unpopularity of television, and the demise of rock music.

But just as Lee had values and principles drilled into him through both his social and his academic education, so too can we drill ourselves. Lee believed in the value of emulation, of learning from great men. As a soldier, he was a student of Napoleon. As an American, his hero was George Washington. And if we find Lee's perfection daunting, we should remember that Lee himself attempted—as indeed every sincere Christian attempts—"the imitation of Christ."

There are two keys to unlocking the secrets of Lee's success as a leader, and they will appear over and over again in his actions throughout this book. The first is his particular Christian worldview. The second is his understanding of the cause for which he fought in the War Between the States.

LEE THE CHRISTIAN

One need only look over the bestseller lists of the last several years to see that many Americans are searching for meaning in their lives through books like *The Celestine Prophecy,* *Chicken Soup for the Soul,* and *All I Really Needed to Know I Learned in Kindergarten.* But a leader is set apart, because he already has a clear view of the world and what he seeks to accomplish in it.

Lee's entire character and persona were tinctured by a devout, deeply injected Anglicanism, the most important content of which, for our purposes, can be separated into two strands.

The Religion of Things As They Are

First, Lee, like Rudyard Kipling, believed in the religion of things as they are. This indeed was a division that separated North from South. In the North, for the descendants of those Pilgrim fathers striving to create shining cities on the hills, religion took on a utopian tilt. Transcendentalism was a phenomenon of the North, arguing that human limits could be overcome by the triumph of individual consciousness. Moreover, as Northern religion became increasingly a religion of rationality—with the rise of Unitarianism—so too did it become politicized. It did not accept the inevitability of Original Sin. It believed that evil could be rooted out and destroyed, that a perfect nation and people could be achieved by zealously pursued reform. One of the first political isms to which this Northern view gave birth was abolitionism. One of its executors was John Brown.

The South, however, lacked a utopian imagination for the simple reason that it didn't believe in Utopia. Transcendentalism never took root because to the Southern mind it was gaseous nonsense that denied the reality of human experience, for which Original Sin was the theological shorthand. Likewise, the South had no interest in "rational religion" because Southerners never had any cause to doubt religion in the first place. The Bible was a road map for navigating the reality of a fallen world. Southerners then, just as "Bible belt" Southerners now, accepted the Bible without question and the fallenness of human nature without complaint. It was just the way things were. Antebellum Southern religion was, in Professor Richard Weaver's words, "a simple acceptance of a body of belief, an innocence of protest and heresy which left religion one of the unquestioned and unquestionable supports of the general settlement under which men live."

In Lee's Virginia especially, the "Cavalier" tradition of the established Episcopal church ensured a broad, easy-going religiosity that accepted the world as it was, that accepted the need for doing good and shunning evil while also recognizing that evil could never be abolished. To think otherwise, to think that man could create heaven on earth, was to be guilty of the sin of pride.

In other words, Lee's religion gave him a profoundly realistic understanding of human nature—essential for any leader.

Lee was a firm believer in the basic Christian tenets, in particular the Christian doctrine of Original Sin. It was a— even *the*—salient point of his character. If he was resolute and confident, if he was never crushed by setbacks or interested in assigning blame for failure, it was because of this. He *expected* men to fail, because, by nature, men usually did. He knew the challenge of leadership was to understand the fallen nature of man and succeed in spite of it.

So far did he believe this—and so far did he feel it was important to understand this reality—that he discouraged his children from reading fiction. In a letter to his wife, he wrote: "Let him [his son Rooney] never touch a novel. They print beauty more charming than nature, and describe happiness that never exists. They will teach him to sigh after that which has no reality, to despise the little good that is granted us in this world and to expect more than is given."

While this view might sound narrow, Lee was no killjoy. On the contrary, he took great pleasure in nature, in his young children, and in the company of charming young women. He felt, rather, that a realistic understanding of life and its limitations—an understanding grounded in an appreciation of Original Sin—provided one with the means to understand and appreciate what was truly good, to enjoy this life we are given of simple pleasures, to keep oneself on a steady keel, and not to allow oneself to wallow amidst unattainable fantasies.

To his son Custis, a cadet at West Point, Lee once wrote: "Shake off those gloomy feelings. Drive them away. Fix your mind and pleasures upon what is before you. . . . All is bright if you will think it so. All is happy if you will make it so. Do not *dream*. It is too ideal, too imaginary. Dreaming by day, I mean. Live in the world you inhabit. Look upon things as they are. Take them as you find them. Make the best of them. Turn them to your advantage."

This philosophy served Lee well in the cauldron of war, where he turned the most inhospitable of circumstances into surprise offensives that stunned his opponents. It was his guiding light in the bleak days of Reconstruction, when his society had been sacked as badly as Rome had been by the barbarians. It was the most fundamental tenet of Lee's view of the world. It is also, in the workaday world, the credo of the successful business leader who accepts the realities imposed by the marketplace—which in themselves can reveal the fallenness of man—and turns them to his advantage.

Self-Discipline

To lead, Lee well understood, one first had to be the master of oneself. Original Sin taught him to expect human failure. But a Christian and a gentleman was obligated to do better. Lee believed that the more one surmounted the baser passions of human nature, the more one approached the divine, the more one successfully imitated Christ, the more one fulfilled one's duty as a Christian gentleman. It was a hierarchical understanding that fit his background and upbringing and that he saw expressed and experienced in the reality of nature, social classes, the army, and the church.

Self-discipline is a basic requirement of effective leadership. That much is a commonplace. If one intends to lead by example and inspire respect, one has to fulfill the ideal of someone whose vision and performance àre coherent, organized, and effective. As Lee said, "I cannot consent to place in the control of others one who cannot control himself."

But the only known way to achieve self-mastery goes against the current of modern American society. That single way, the narrow gate through which effective leaders must pass, was expressed by Lee after the war when he advised a mother on the instruction of her infant son: "Teach him he must deny himself."

In our own age, we might expect an educator to say: "Teach him self-expression" or "Teach him self-esteem." And, at first blush, teaching a business leader to deny himself might seem at odds with the very nature of capitalism, which seeks to fulfill and inflame material wants.

But business, like war, can be a perilous undertaking, with livelihoods—if not lives themselves—at stake. In business as in war success is often given to the best disciplined, the toughest, and the most prepared.

A successful business leader must be self-disciplined. He needs to put hard work before leisure; to put the desires of his customers for a high-quality, low-priced product ahead of his own desire for a cheaply produced, high-priced product. He needs to lead by a personal example that inspires employees rather than by a personal convenience that makes them cynical and ready to trim corners or cut and run to another employer. He needs to understand, as a plaque on Ronald Reagan's desk in the Oval Office read, that "There is no limit to what a man can do or where he can go if he doesn't mind who gets the credit."

That sentiment was well-ingrained in Lee. The leadership challenge he faced in the War Between the States was exacerbated not only by the circumstances of attempting to create a new army practically overnight—and in the face of imminent invasion by a much larger, much richer, much more industrialized foe—but because the Southern society for which Lee fought was full of hot-headed, hot-blooded individualists, especially in the officer corps, which was dominated by status-seeking West Point–educated officers, former governors, wealthy planters, academics, lawyers, self-made businessmen, and the occasional fighting bishop. They were men used to command. The Confederate troops were largely independent-minded small-time farmers used to governing themselves. They were not industrial workers used to being ordered around by a boss, or in this case, by an officer. The Confederacy for which they fought not only jealously protected their individual rights—including the right, in many cases, to elect their own officers—but the rights and prerogatives of their separate states.

Lee was followed by these fractious, states-rights, individualistic Southerners not because he enforced draconian discipline on *them,* but because he exemplified it in his own behavior. Lee was recognized as a leader by right of his *character.* Part of that character was his sense of realism, which inspired trust, and his like-minded trust in his men, which inspired confidence. Lee believed that officers, as gentlemen, should be able to govern themselves, and by their example, so should their men.

To his soldiers, Lee was remarkable; his self-mastery fed their awe. They knew him as a ferociously aggressive commander who never swore and rarely lost his temper; he was too fiercely focused on the matter at hand—fighting and winning, *their common goal*—to waste his energies on choler or abuse. He shared the privations of the common soldier, but he did not share his weaknesses. Though under tremendous stress, he never sought escape through John Barleycorn. For all he suffered, he was immune to self-pity. As famous as he became, he shunned self-advertisement. A hero, he avoided public appearances, except as dictated by duty and good manners.

As Lee's Pulitzer Prize–winning biographer Douglas Southall Freeman wrote: "Had his life been epitomized in one sentence of the Book he read so often, it would have been in the words, 'If any man will come after me, let him deny himself, and take up his cross daily, and follow me.'" If Lee had an example of perfect leadership, it was in the man that he most wanted to follow himself, the God-Man of the New Testament. From Him, and from the social tradition of noblesse oblige in which Lee was raised, Lee developed a particular abhorrence of selfishness.

Again, this might seem an unlikely attribute for business leaders—caricatured in popular culture as belonging to the "greed is good" school of philosophy. Certainly it is an unpopular view in our own time when the marketplace is devoted to the fulfillment of self, when self-fulfillment is seen as a worthy—perhaps the most worthy—goal, when it is a popular cliché that one's paramount duty is "the duty I owe myself," when courses are taught in "self-assertion," when a magazine can proudly claim the title *Self*, and when the very goal of leadership and business success appears to be the achievement of selfish desires.

But Lee's was a more prudent and mature view, and for the would-be leader, a more practical one. He recognized that most men—especially soldiers—have every reason to regard selfishness as a vice, and to regard an officer who thinks first of himself and then of his men, who is casual about *their* lives and well-being but selfishly protective of his own, as unworthy of his commission. Vice, however tempting to the individual, rarely invites respect in practice. Leaders who lack the respect of their subordinates must rely on force—something

Lee regarded with acute distaste and as a confession of failure, necessary only under the most extreme circumstances. For the modern business leader it might also be appropriate to point out that leaders who rely on force are ultimately ineffective businessmen—especially in a competitive marketplace operating with a free exchange of labor and capital.

Lee did not, of course, travel the country giving seminars on leadership or advertise himself as a management guru with a ten-step plan to business success. He did not lecture about leadership—he practiced it. He set a personal example of the devotion to duty he desired of his officers and his men. As befit one born to a landed aristocracy that felt set above and therefore responsible for the common people with whom it interacted in business and other pursuits, he felt "the great duty of life" was "the promotion of the happiness and welfare" of others. As an officer, the great duty was "looking after the men." As a military strategist, it was to achieve, by analogy, the same goal, matching "easy fighting and heavy victories." In a business sense, it would mean putting the demands of one's customers and the treatment of one's employees ahead of thoughts of oneself.

Lee followed this "great duty" throughout his life, not just in his public responsibilities as an officer and an educator but, perhaps even more telling, in his private life—where so many contemporary leaders tend to cut corners, thinking leadership is something one delivers in a speech rather than something one embodies in one's character. As a young man, Lee took on the responsibility of nursing his mother until her death, and later of nursing his wife, whose health faltered in her late twenties and who was crippled by arthritis before she was fifty. He never used another's suffering as an excuse, as Black Horse Harry Lee had done, to indulge his passions elsewhere, or to allow feelings of frustration to overcome him.

He disciplined himself to accept things as they were, to do his duty cheerfully because there was no sense in doing it any other way, and to do what he thought right without expectation of reward or recognition. In his own words, it was enough to have "the satisfaction that proceeds from the consciousness of duty faithfully performed." It is the goal of every business leader to inspire just such an ethos in his employees.

WHAT HE FOUGHT FOR

In the War Between the States—the tremendous calamity that propelled Lee into the national consciousness—Lee fought for the Confederate States of America, for a new nation breaking away from the United States, just as his father had fought for a new nation breaking away from Mother England. While fighting on the side of slave-holding states seceding from the Union, Lee fought neither for the right to own slaves nor even for the right to secession. Indeed, he regarded the latter as "nothing less than revolution"—and Lee was not a revolutionary. As for slavery, Lee had his entire life believed in gradual emancipation. In his own affairs, he had no slaves of his own and freed every slave he inherited from his father-in-law's estate *before* the Union attempted to enforce the Emancipation Proclamation on the seceded Southern states. More than that, he made every effort to ensure that the slaves under his care were freed under circumstances where they could support themselves—a step he believed that abolitionists, driven by zealotry, failed to consider.

Perhaps more surprising is that Lee privately counseled Confederate President Jefferson Davis "often and early in the war that the slaves should be emancipated" and urged upon him a presidential "proclamation of gradual emancipation" that would have allowed "the use of . . . negroes as soldiers" in the Confederate army.

Lee's most famous statement on slavery came in a letter he wrote to his wife shortly after Christmas 1856, while he was away from his Virginia home on duty in Texas. "In this enlightened age," he wrote, "there are few I believe, but what will acknowledge, that slavery as an institution, is a moral and political evil in any Country. It is useless to expatiate on its disadvantages. I think it however a greater evil to the white than to the black race."

The latter statement is particularly interesting for our own purposes for what it says about Lee's view of leadership and power. Power, Lee implied—and certainly believed—can corrupt. The famous axiom to that effect was coined by Lord Acton, who corresponded with Lee after the war and who was sympathetic to the Confederacy, believing its devotion to states rights was a necessary check on "the absolutism of the sovereign will."

But just as power corrupts—the corruption making slavery ultimately "a greater evil to the white than to the black race"—so too, in Lee's view, did the *lack* of responsibility corrupt the abolitionists who agitated for an immediate end to slavery. Lee believed that they did not consider the consequences of their agitation (which, of course, helped propel the country to war), or understand that the relationship between master and slave *could be*—and *had been,* in his experience—conducted within a Christian framework, moderated by the kindness that masters in the New Testament were instructed to show their slaves.

Southern slaveholders would be better and more justly convinced of the rightness of gradual emancipation, in Lee's view, by gentle persuasion rather than by force, which he thought extremist, unjustified, unconstitutional, and un-Christian. Lee held that Christianity's "mild and melting influence" would sooner rectify slavery's evils than would the "storms and tempests of fiery controversy," which might make them worse by stirring up ill-feeling. "Is it not strange," Lee wrote with rare sarcasm, "that the descendants of those pilgrim fathers who Crossed the Atlantic to preserve their own freedom of opinion, have always proved themselves intolerant of the Spiritual liberty of others?"

The religious division between the New England Puritan eager to exorcise sin and the tolerant, latitudinarian Virginian Cavalier content with the slow progress of Providence, was raised once again.

But if Lee fought not for the expansion of slavery or for secession, what did he fight for? Why did he consent to turn his back on the flag that he had sworn to defend as a cadet at West Point, that he had spent his entire professional life defending, that he was committed to as a patriot, the son of patriots, a veteran of the Mexican War, and the father and uncle of West Point cadets?

Lee was a conservative, dedicated to the Old Republic, and opposed to violent change, whether it came from the rhetoric of fire-breathing secessionists on the one hand or would-be leaders of a slave rebellion on the other. Lee's preference was for things to stay as they were, for political arguments to be settled by the established process of debate, compromise, and legislation rather than by force, and for slavery—as a national evil and source of political contention—to be gradually erased by prudent, respectful moral suasion, not by bloodshed.

But it was not to be. Secessionist passions came to a boil when South Carolina left the Union in December 1860, fed up with federal tariffs that hurt its free trade–driven economy and federal interference in what the Palmetto State regarded as its sovereign affairs. In South Carolinian eyes, the election of Abraham Lincoln (who failed to carry a single Southern or border state) meant an exacerbation of regional disputes, with the North now gaining the upper hand. South Carolina was better off outside the Union than in it—or so its secessionist leaders proclaimed. By February 1861, South Carolina had been followed by Mississippi, Alabama, Georgia, Louisiana, Florida, and Texas, with these states joining to form a provisional government and a new country, the national capital of which would be in Montgomery, Alabama.

The states of the upper South, however, still hoped for a political compromise and a peaceful resolution to the crisis. It was not until President Lincoln ordered Virginia, North Carolina, Tennessee, and Arkansas to provide troops to suppress the rebellious states of the lower South that the die was cast. The elected representatives of these states did not believe that armed force was an acceptable route to political compromise.

Lee's decision of where his duty lay was made for him by Virginia's refusal to wage war against her fellow Southern states. His ultimate loyalty was to Virginia, and while Lee had opposed secession, he conceded that "a Union that can only be maintained by swords and bayonets . . . has no charm for me."

It may have lacked charm, but it also came with the promise of power, promotion, and fame. As war became increasingly inevitable, Lee was called to the home of Francis P. Blair, a confidant of the new Lincoln administration. Blair said he was authorized to offer Lee command of the new army being formed to take action against the South. It was America's highest field command, and Lee would have the gratitude of the president and an unparalleled opportunity for glory and reward.

But Lee respectfully declined. He replied that "though opposed to secession . . . I could take no part in the invasion of the Southern states." After his interview with Blair, Lee visited his former commander, General Winfield Scott, the senior officer in the Army, and informed him of his decision. "Lee, you have made the greatest mistake of your life," Scott replied. "But I feared it would be so."

For Lee the issue was simple, even if the decision had been reached, in his wife's words, with "tears of blood." "With all my devotion to the Union," Lee wrote, "and the feeling of loyalty and duty as an American citizen, I have not been able to make up my mind to raise my hand against my relatives, my children, my home."

"I shall return to my native state," Lee wrote in another, earlier letter, "and share the miseries of my people, and save in defense will draw my sword on none."

These were words not only of familial feeling and of patriotism to Virginia, they were words of direct homage to his father, who had himself declared, "Virginia is my country. Her will I obey, however lamentable the fate to which it may subject me."

Virginia's fate turned out to be lamentable indeed. But for Robert E. Lee—as for Socrates, whose lessons Lee had absorbed in his classical schooling—it was better to suffer evil than to commit it. Lee rode to the defense of his state, his family, and his friends. He could do no less and still regard himself as an honorable man. He would not consent to butcher his fellow Virginians, and those who attempted to do so for the political ideal of the Union, who relied on force rather than persuasion, who had exposed the hypocrisy of their professed belief in the rights of a people to determine their own government, could only be referred to, through clenched teeth, as "those people."

If Lee's decision is controversial now, it was, of course, much more controversial *then*, when more than "political correctness" was at stake. Men's lives were in the balance, as was the life of the Union and the life of a new, embattled confederated republic. Unlike those who assumed the South's independence was assured and would be easily maintained against the Federals, Lee, in the words of his aide Walter Taylor, "looked upon the vaporific declamations of those on each side who proposed to wipe their adversaries from the face of the earth in ninety days as bombastic and foolish." That was Lee the realist.

He also remained Lee the tolerant Anglican, who allowed others—even his own blood relations, his sons—untrammeled freedom to pursue the dictates of conscience. Lee wrote his wife that their son Custis "must consult his own judgment, reason and conscience as to the course he may take. I do not wish him to be guided by my wishes or example. If I have done wrong, let him do better."

This trust in conscience—and in the guiding hand of Providence—was another of Lee's great strengths. By following his conscience, by doing what he honestly thought was right, by straining every sinew to achieve that right as dictated by duty, he guaranteed himself the serene self-confidence that is necessary in a leader. He expressed himself on this point in a letter to his daughter Mildred: "The struggle which you describe you experience between doing what you ought and what you desire is common to all. You have only always to do what is right. It will become easier by practice, and you will enjoy in the midst of your trials the pleasure of an approving conscience. That will be worth everything else."

By trusting to Providence, he knew that even the worst outcomes would somehow be turned to right. As he told the Reverend J. William Jones, who could not give up thinking that the late war might have been won if certain decisions had been made at key points, "Yes, all that is very sad, and might be a cause for self-reproach, but that we are conscious that we have humbly tried to do our duty. We may therefore, with calm satisfaction, trust in God and leave the results to Him."

If Lee were to address a meeting of young business presidents today, there is no doubt what he would tell them: Look after your people, do what is right, fulfill your duty to the best of your ability, and take confidence in the judgment of Providence, leaving the results to God.

As we will see, these guiding principles led Lee to victory in combat, to triumph over apparent defeat, and to heroism in war and peace.

LEE'S LESSONS

* Accept life as it is and make the best of it. "Live in the world you inhabit. Look upon things as they are. Take them as you find them. Make the best of them. Turn them to your advantage."

* To lead others, one must first master oneself. "I cannot consent to place in the control of others one who cannot control himself."

* A leader's primary responsibility is to think of others first. The "great duty of life" is "the promotion of the happiness and welfare of our fellow men."

* A leader should always do what conscience dictates so he will never have cause for self-doubt. "You have only always to do what is right. It will become easier by practice, and you will enjoy in the midst of your trials the pleasure of an approving conscience. That will be worth everything else."

CHAPTER TWO

APPRENTICESHIP
IN MEXICO

UNTIL HE WAS forty years old, Robert E. Lee was employed by the United States Army as an engineer. His job was to build things. He constructed forts, served as assistant to the chief of the Engineer Department in Washington, and diverted the Mississippi River for the benefit of the harbor in St. Louis. Each of these experiences would prove useful. Construction taught Lee how to manage men and supplies. At his desk job in Washington, Lee learned how to push paper—something he hated to do throughout his life, but which he learned to do expeditiously whenever he could not, as a commanding general, delegate it to others. Perhaps most interesting, as an engineer on the Mississippi, Lee's strategy for building a dyke and dam relied on simple construction but also on using the power of the river to sweep driftwood to the support of his structures and to push an encroaching sandbar, which threatened to block the St. Louis harbor, out of the way. It was judo on the Mississippi, working *with* the force of nature, directing its power to his own uses rather than fighting against it. It was the kind of strategic thinking that Lee would exhibit repeatedly in war, and that he had recommended to his son Custis:

Take things as you find them. "Make the best of them. Turn them to your advantage."

With the outbreak of war with Mexico in 1846, Lee received new assignments. In Mexico, the army's greatest need was not for the construction of roads or bridges—though there were some construction projects of that kind—but for accurate reconnaissance in the absence of reliable maps. Engineers were thought particularly suited for this duty, and Lee became a scout, often rising as early as three hours before dawn and covering 50 to 60 miles a day on horseback.

FUNDAMENTALS OF LEADERSHIP: COURAGE, INTELLIGENCE, PERSEVERANCE, RESPONSIBILITY

Lee had yet to come under fire, but he had already proved himself perdurable and courageous. When reports came of a large Mexican force heading toward the Americans, Lee volunteered to investigate. He took a young Mexican as his guide, and the two rode far into the twilight. At one point they saw flickering campfires amidst a scattering of white dots in the distance. Lee's guide immediately recognized the dots as Mexican army tents and recommended a hasty retreat. Lee, however, rode forward alone to discover that the tents were, in fact, sheep. The fires were the campfires of their drovers, who willingly told Lee the disposition of the Mexican force on the other side of the mountains. Lee set off on another marathon ride to find the enemy, and did so, reporting its less than threatening position to his commanding officer, the felicitously named General John E. Wool.

In January 1847, Lee received orders for a new assignment at the headquarters of General Winfield Scott, for whom he became a staff officer. It was here, too, that he was first shot at: returning to the American lines after digging forward entrenchments for the artillery, a nervous American soldier, mistaking Lee for an advancing Mexican, fired his pistol at him, the ball of "friendly fire" passing between Lee's arm and his body, singeing his uniform.

Lee's new assignment had him continuing his detailed reconnaissance work, but also placing and directing artillery and sitting in on General Scott's councils of war. He saw his first action at the battle of Vera Cruz. There he was joined by his older brother Smith Lee, a navy officer in charge of naval batteries that were brought on land to join the army's artillery in assaulting the city. Robert was untroubled by the danger to his own life, but he did worry about his brother. "No matter where I turned, my eyes reverted to him, and I stood by his gun whenever I was not wanted elsewhere. Oh! I felt awfully, and am at a loss what I should have done had he been cut down before me. I thank God that he was saved. He preserved his usual cheerfulness, and I could see his white teeth through all the smoke and din of the fire."

It seems odd reading this that Robert E. Lee was the *younger* brother, such is his sense of responsibility for Smith Lee. But this sense of responsibility was a hallmark of his life. He was the fatherless boy who was remembered for being cheerful, helpful, and frugal; he was the model cadet, studious, responsible, thoughtful, who never earned a single demerit for bad behavior; he was the devoted son, freshly minted from West Point, who cared for his mother through her last days.

Lee was a leader because he never shrank from his duty, because he accepted responsibility, because he always did what conscience dictated. He was a leader even when he was a subordinate, happily accepting the responsibilities of those senior to himself.

Lee was cool under fire—"I am thankful I have so far stood it"—but he was under no illusions as to its effects. He took responsibility for that too. He grieved for his dead colleagues, "the fine fellows," but even more for the Mexican civilians who had been caught in the city: "My heart bled for the inhabitants . . . it was terrible to think of the women and children."

Lee thought of them often and later in his career took pains to avoid civilian casualties. In 1859, for example, Colonel Robert E. Lee was ordered to arrest John Brown and his band of violent abolitionists, who had attempted to capture the arsenal at Harper's Ferry, Virginia (now West Virginia), as a precursor to launching a slave rebellion. Brown had occupied the Harper's Ferry firehouse and taken hostages. Lee instructed the U.S. Marines under his command to attack the firehouse with sledgehammers (to break into it) and bayonets. But the Marines' rifles were unloaded in order to avoid civilian casualties. By Lee's standards, the civilized use of armed force required the Marines *not* to take extra precautions for their own safety—by loading their guns—which might unduly endanger the lives of Brown's civilian hostages.

Lee always took care to keep his means, the use of force, appropriate to his ends—in this case the freeing of hostages and the arrest of the insurrectionist John Brown. As a leader, he shouldered the responsibility for ensuring that objectives were achieved with a minimum of collateral damage.

Similarly, in the War Between the States, he took responsibility for ensuring that his men's actions were guided by firm moral principles that were inviolable even under provocation or the passion of self-interest. At the outset of his Maryland campaign in 1862, Lee issued his famous General Orders No. 73, reminding his troops that while Union soldiers might set Southern farms ablaze, the Confederate Army would not wage war on civilians:

> The commanding general considers that no greater disgrace could befall the army . . . than the perpetration of the bar-

barous outrages upon the unarmed and defenseless, and the wanton destruction of private property that have marked the course of the enemy in our own country. . . .

It must be remembered that we make war only upon armed men, and that we cannot take vengeance for the wrongs our people have suffered without offending against Him to whom vengeance belongeth, without whose favor and support our efforts must all prove in vain.

War might be hell, as Union General William Tecumseh Sherman famously observed ("War is cruelty, you cannot refine it"), but he saw no reason to make it more so. After Gettysburg, Lee wrote to his wife that however much the Union army waged war on Southern civilians, their homes, and their livelihoods, "I do not think we should follow their example. The consequences of war are horrid enough at best, surrounded by all the amelioration of civilization and Christianity. Why should we aggravate them?"

For Lee the soldier, war—the controlled use of force for political objectives—might be necessary to achieve a greater good, but its violence should be contained. For the business leader as much as the military officer, the lesson is the same: a leader is responsible for the consequences of his actions, and he should seek to minimize damage. For the officer it means avoiding civilian casualties. For the business leader, it means ensuring that the "creative destruction" of capitalism—of innovation and change—does not degenerate into simple destruction per se. This might mean anything from tightening pollution controls (if environmental pollution is an inevitable by-product of one's industry) to minimizing the economic consequences of necessary corporate layoffs on employee families and their community to simply taking any action within one's power to avoid causing harm in the process of achieving one's business objectives. More subtly, but just as important, it should include refusing to invest in products that are socially harmful and assuring that humane and worthy traditions are not needlessly sacrificed to efficiency, utilitarianism, or the worship of the *new*.

In the Mexican War, Lee was still a captain, not a general, and the newly blooded officer was focused on executing his orders and endeavoring "to perform what little service I can to my country." The most important of these services was his reconnaissance work, for which Lee's cool-headedness, his sharp eye for geography, and his physical powers of endurance well suited him. In one instance, Lee was left hiding beneath a large tree trunk for the better part of a day, as Mexican troops gathered and even sat on the very log that hid him.

Lee repaid the Mexicans for his discomfort by renewing his reconnaissance and navigating a maze of ravines, where he discovered a way for the American army to swing behind the Mexicans, driving them from their position at Cerro Gordo. For his role in this battle, General Scott mentioned Lee in his dispatches—calling him "indefatigable. . . . Nor was he less conspicuous in planting batteries, and in conducting columns to their stations under the heavy fire of the enemy."

Lee was eager for the clash of combat. He wrote that his horse, Creole, "stepped over the dead men with such care as if she feared to hurt them, but when I started with the dragoons in the pursuit, she was as fierce as possible, and I could barely hold her." Creole sounds much like Lee himself.

But however hot the blood in the chase and in the fight, Lee remained the Christian soldier. He wrote his son Custis after the battle, "You have no idea what a horrible sight a battlefield is." He told him how he had come across a dying Mexican soldier sprawled across a wounded boy—the boy coming to his attention by the crying of a Mexican girl. "Her large black eyes were streaming with tears, her hands crossed over her breast; her hair in one long plait behind reached her waist, her shoulders and arms bare, and without stockings or shoes. Her plaintive tone of '*Millie gracias, Signor,*' as I had the dying man lifted off the boy and both carried to the hospital still lingers in my ear."

Lee's most famous feat in the Mexican war was guiding American troops into action through the *pedregal,* a bed of lava five miles wide, apparently impassable, that blocked the American advance to Mexico City. Roads ran along either side of the *pedregal,* but these were easily and heavily defended. Undaunted, Lee penetrated the volcanic rock field and not only found a passage but led three brigades through and into action against the enemy's rear, delivering victory at the battle of Contreras. He then retraced his route to Scott's headquarters and guided troops to a flank attack in the battle of Churubusco, chasing the Mexicans from the field. The battles punctuated nearly 40 consecutive hours of wakeful action by Lee.

In his after-battle report, General Persifor Smith noted that Lee's "reconnaissances, though carried far beyond the bounds of prudence, were conducted with so much skill that their fruits were of the utmost value, the soundness of his judgment and his personal daring being equally conspicuous." General Winfield Scott thought Lee's performance "the greatest feat of physical and moral courage performed by any individual in my knowledge." He referred to the "gallant, indefatigable Captain Lee" who was "as distinguished for felicitous execution as for science and daring."

There was that word "indefatigable" again. It came up often in descriptions of Lee's conduct. Even Lee himself, who was not given to boasting, felt compelled to notice in a letter to his wife that there "are few men more healthy or more able to bear exposure and fatigue, nor do I know of any of my present associates that have undergone as much of either in this campaign." But even the "gallant, indefatigable Lee" could be pushed beyond human limits. General Scott had by now, in the words of General Erasmus D. Keyes, an "almost idolatrous fancy for Lee, whose military ability he estimated far beyond that of any other officer of the army," and he intended to use him to the fullest.

LEARN FROM YOUR SUPERIORS— AND FROM EXPERIENCE

In the age of Dilbert, it will probably not surprise readers to learn that Lee suffered from "the curse of competence"—or perhaps more accurately, the curse of competence when noted by one's superiors. Lee was now called upon to do more than one man could. In the assault on Chapultepec, before the occupation of Mexico City, Lee was retained by Scott with responsibility for executing "his directions and bringing him news of the events of the day." In other words, Lee had to be all over the field, placing artillery, bringing reports to General Scott, then riding off on reconnaissance. At some point Lee sustained a flesh wound, and after nearly 60 hours of sleepless action, he found "I could no longer keep my saddle" and collapsed, bleeding and exhausted. After a brief rest, he recovered well enough to ride the next morning into Mexico City as one of the conquering heroes of the American army— indeed as "the very best soldier" General Winfield Scott "ever saw in the field."

Scott's ranking of Lee as a "military genius" is noteworthy because Scott himself was the finest American military intellect of his time. Serving on his staff was a profound educational experience for Lee. Lee noted how Scott assessed information and transformed reconnaissance reports into plans of action; how he favored bold maneuvers that took huge risks; how he gave no thought to retreat; how he developed strategic approaches and objectives, but left the execution to his subordinates.

Known as "Old Fuss and Feathers," Scott had a huge appetite for food, pomp, and fame. His character was far different from Lee's, but Lee admired Scott's generalship and adopted much of his military program as his own. Lee, too, would prove an audacious commander, willing to risk all to win all. He, too, would rely heavily on his corps commanders to execute his strategy, expecting them to seize opportunities as battle developed.

There were other lessons, as well. In an army that was part volunteer, part professional, Scott chose West Pointers as his staff officers. In the War Between the States, Lee would show a similar preference for experienced officers from the regular army.

Lee would also never forget the lessons of his own reconnaissance—it was vital to know the ground. With that knowledge one could outflank the enemy and defeat him by maneuver, rather than by direct approaches and mutual slaughter.

More basic than anything else, Lee had seen combat. He had put all his academic training into action, placing guns, assessing and destroying enemy fortifications, scouting enemy dispositions, and leading American troops into hostile fire.

Though a career officer, Lee entered the Mexican War in many ways still an apprentice, untouched by battle. He left it a professional, sure of his abilities and tested in command. Lee's rite of passage is one that all leaders must undergo. A history of success under fire is what turns a potential leader into an active one, and what most powerfully justifies a leader to those he leads.

It would be another 14 years before Lee would put his leadership lessons to full use, and in that titanic struggle over the fate of the Union and for the survival of the newborn

Confederate States of America, he would lead and confront men who had learned their own lessons in the Mexican desert—men like Thomas J. Jackson, Joseph E. Johnston, Pierre Gustave Toutant Beauregard, James Longstreet, George B. McClellan, and most fatefully of all, Ulysses S. Grant.

LEE'S LESSONS

• Know the ground. A leader must have a firm, clear grasp of his field so that he can outmaneuver his opponents.

• Do your own reconnaissance. A leader uses his own eyes and ears to investigate facts whenever possible. One true mark of a leader is the courage to pursue information to its logical conclusion and to have the cool-headed, clear-eyed good judgment not to mistake sheep for soldiers.

• Be indefatigable. A leader must have the endurance to out-think and outlast his opponents, and to take the hard road when it is the right road.

• Learn from your superiors. Leadership can be learned from successful executives far different from oneself in temperament. Copy a successful leader's techniques and learn from his mistakes.

• Leadership is legitimized by success under fire. To be a leader, one cannot wait on the sidelines. One has to take responsibility, enter the fray, and prove that one has the resourcefulness, ability, and character to get things done.

• Leadership requires moral responsibility. A leader is responsible not only for his own actions but for those of his subordinates and for the overall effect of his enterprise.

CHAPTER THREE

LEE, THE BUSINESSMAN

LIKE MANY OF US, Lee yearned for a quiet life. His constant wish was to farm an isolated piece of land in Virginia. That wish was never granted. But in the years before the War Between the States, Lee did inherit the responsibility for running Arlington plantation, which was willed to his wife. His challenge was to do it successfully enough to pay off his father-in-law's debts and to finance the bequests he had willed to Lee's daughters. So Lee became a businessman.

His task wasn't easy, and he had to work against a ticking clock. The slaves on Arlington plantation were not the abused victims of *Uncle Tom's Cabin.* Their owner, George Washington's step-grandson Washington Custis, had been a man with little interest in business—either in working himself, or in seeing others work. Moreover, like George Washington, Thomas Jefferson, and other aristocratic Virginians, Washington Custis thought that slavery was something that succeeding generations should find a way to do without, so his will mandated that his slaves be emancipated within five years of his death.

Robert E. Lee, therefore, inherited the challenge of rebuilding a neglected property, turning its fallow fields to profitable farming, and doing so quickly with unmotivated laborers who had no stake in Arlington's future, who were unused to hard work, and who now considered themselves "short-timers" who would soon be doing something else, something easier, something more personally rewarding.

Lee, of course, had no training as a businessman, but he employed the principles he had learned as an engineer and as a soldier to become a successful farmer. He defined his objective—retiring Washington Custis's $10,000 in debt and raising the $40,000 he had willed, but not set aside, for Lee's daughters. He assessed his means—his property and his inherited slaves, soon to be manumitted. He surveyed the difficulties— the inherited debt, a run-down estate, and a surly, lackadaisical workforce who didn't care one whit for his objectives.

Lee, the business leader, took action, tackling each problem individually, systematically clearing away obstacles, eliminating wasteful expenditure, revitalizing neglected assets, and moving Arlington's accounts inexorably from the red to the black.

HARD WORK AND FRUGALITY

Lee's experience as an engineer had inured him to hard projects. As Douglas Southall Freeman wrote: "His engineering work was not always interesting but it usually was troublesome. . . . He spent so many days in mud and water up to his armpits, that a certain interested young woman . . . wondered how he survived it, and to the end of her days never ceased to marvel at it."

Unlike his father-in-law, Lee was unafraid of hard work. When Lee worked on the Mississippi River, the mayor of Saint Louis recorded his efforts:

> [Lee] went in person with the hands every morning about sunrise, and worked day by day in the hot broiling sun,—the heat

being greatly increased by the reflection of the river. He shared the hard task and the common fare and rations furnished to the common laborers,—eating at the same table, in the cabin of the steamboat used in the prosecution of the work, but never on any occasion becoming too familiar with the men. He maintained and preserved under all circumstances his dignity and gentlemanly bearing, winning and commanding the esteem, regard, and respect of every one under him. He also slept in the cabin of the steamboat, moored to the bank near the works . . . [and] worked at his drawings, plans and estimates every night till 11 o'clock.

Lee's later performance in the Mexican War proved that his powers of physical endurance had not faded with age. Nor did his capacity for hard work fail him in the massive project of restoring Arlington's fortunes.

But Lee was used to directing soldiers, not slaves; and with his own qualms about the "peculiar institution" he did not particularly relish the prospect of having to deal with restive field hands who felt they owed him no loyalty. To deal with this difficulty, Lee adopted the expedient of treating inefficient slaves the same way he would later treat inefficient officers—he transferred them. Or more specifically, he rented the slaves to small planters, earning cash while relieving himself of the grumblers.

He also made other reforms. By nature, Lee believed in governing with an easy hand. Indeed, he operated on the reverse of Machiavelli's dictum that it is better to be feared than to be loved. During the War Between the States, he continually reminded his officers to look after the men, and likewise, during his administration of Arlington, slaves who were willing to work were treated generously. He believed in giving them "every aid and comfort" so "they will be the happier."

He also rebuilt the overseer's house, which had fallen into disgraceful dilapidation. He sold Custis's unprofitable stock of horses and cattle, and rented Arlington's mill to a miller who knew what to do with it. Like a corporate streamliner, Lee focused Arlington plantation on what he regarded as its core business—growing corn and wheat.

Supervising the renovation of buildings and the planting of fields during the day, he spent his nights poring over Arlington's accounts. He had been raised the frugal son of a family that had had frugality forced upon it, and he imposed the same financial discipline on the plantation's operations. Well before he would think of putting money aside for his daughters, Lee conscientiously made settling Custis's debts the first goal to be met by Arlington profits.

Financial responsibility was, in Lee's view, merely another duty that a good man must happily and dedicatedly accept. As Lee would later advise his newlywed son Rooney, "I hope you will continue *never to exceed your means*. It will save you much anxiety and mortification and enable you to maintain your independence of character and feeling." This was a crucial point for Lee: he believed that freedom came not from self-indulgence but from self-restraint and probity.

Lee had, of course, the hard lesson of his father's imprisonment and later self-imposed exile due to debt. But he also agreed with Edmund Burke that men's passions—including the passion to spend beyond their means—forged their fetters. If one restrained passion, one was free. One might expect a common man to be hobbled—indeed, one *saw* him hobbled—by all manner of passions. But it was the mark of a gentleman and a leader to rise above passion, to practice Christian self-restraint, to follow the straight line of duty that led to contentment, and to be too wise for the colorful carnivals of vanity fair that attracted the mob and shackled them with heavy chains of debt, debility, and degradation. Lee concluded: "It is easier"—and of course better—"to make our wishes conform to our means than to make our means conform to our wishes."

Lee's realism extended to recognizing that the businessmen he dealt with had their own success uppermost in mind, not his. While he detested few things more than selfishness, he understood that business, by its nature, is a congeries of thrusting self-interests. As he wrote his eldest son, Custis Lee, "You must be aware of one thing, that those you deal with will consider their advantage and not yours. So while being fair and just, you must not neglect your interests." Douglas Southall Freeman notes that all "his life Lee had lived with gentle people." There is no better reminder of it, and of the Virginia tradition in which he was raised, than Lee's gentle admonition to his son that in business, "while being fair and just," it was all right to think of oneself once in a while.

ORGANIZING THE DAY

Self-interest, for Lee, always spilled over into self-management. For a leader, self-management can mean many things, but primary among them is organizing the day to seize irreplaceable time. Lee organized his day according to three principles.

First, he believed in getting the day's work done in the day allotted, even if the day's work included a mass of hateful paper-pushing. As his staff officer Walter Taylor wrote: "His correspondence, necessarily heavy, was constantly a source of worry and annoyance to him. He did not enjoy writing; indeed he wrote with labor, and nothing seemed to tax his amiability so much as the necessity for writing a lengthy official communication; but he was not satisfied unless at the close of his office hours every matter requiring prompt attention had been disposed of."

Lee's punctiliousness about clearing his desk reflected his belief that an effective leader had to be a good administrator. As Douglas Southall Freeman noted, Lee's nearest "rule of thumb for judging the competence of an officer was the condition in which he found that officer's camp. Other things being even, he assumed that a good army administrator is going to be a good combat officer. He reasoned in this wise: If a man is not careful in camp, how can we assume that that man will be careful on the field of battle?" So, too, for a business leader in judging his subordinates, a clean desk might very well be the sign of a self-disciplined, effective, organized mind.

Second, Lee believed in going to bed by 10 P.M., if possible, and starting the day early. Freeman relates that Lee held to the theory that an hour's sleep *before* midnight was worth at least two hours sleep *after* midnight. During the War Between the States, Lee was frequently in his saddle hours before dawn to steal a march on the enemy. He also liked to issue the day's communiqués, orders, and reports before breakfast, clearing out paperwork so he could devote the majority of his daylight hours to assessing movements in the field.

Retiring early was perhaps a lesson in self-discipline he had learned in Mexico when he had pushed himself to the point of collapse. By forcing himself to rest well before midnight, an officer avoids the temptation to go without sleep, ensuring his capacity for a long campaign.

Third, Lee knew the importance of coming up for air, of taking time out for exercise and reflection. Whenever possible, he set aside half an hour or so in the afternoon to ride on horseback into the country—or if a horse wasn't available, then to walk—to clear his mind of current, pressing duties and to focus on the beauties of nature, which he well appreciated. Later in his life he confessed, "I do not see how I could have stood what I had to go through" without his sojourns on his favorite mount, Traveller. These quiet periods on horse-back did for Robert E. Lee what afternoon naps did for Winston Churchill—they reinvigorated him to meet the challenges of the rest of the day. It was not time wasted. For effective use of the remains of the day, it was time *restored*.

Lee took two years' leave from the army to untangle Washington Custis's estate, to put Arlington back in working order, and to generate money to discharge his father-in-law's debts. In those two years, he proved himself a successful planter and businessman. But when the army called him to Texas to chase Indians and Mexican bandits, he went willingly, finding military duty—even far from his family and his beloved Virginia—less onerous than cleaning up after another's financial folly.

Soon, however, all Lee's good work in restoring Arlington would be undone. His wife's familial home—his home, as well, for many years—sat majestically above the Potomac River, the blue ribbon of water that would soon divide North and South. After the first shots of the war, Arlington House would be occupied and laid waste. Mary Lee's property would be seized by the Federal government. The inherited effects of George Washington that had been passed through her family would be stolen. And Arlington's fertile fields would become a national cemetery.

LEE'S LESSONS

• An effective leader is an effective administrator. Finish the day's work in the day allotted, maintain an orderly camp (or more likely, office), and while sharing "the hard task and the common fare" of one's subordinates and adding on top of it the responsibilities of paperwork and supervision, make time for rest, recreation, and reflection. This is not time wasted, but time restored.

• A leader knows that "men's passions forge their fetters." A leader controls his passions and his appetites; they do not control him.

• A leader is free to act so far as he is free from debt. A leader keeps his objectives consistent with his means.

CHAPTER FOUR

LEE, THE STRATEGIST

LIGHT HORSE HARRY LEE had famously eulogized his friend George Washington as "first in war, first in peace, and first in the hearts of his countrymen."

Now Robert E. Lee stood in the Virginia House of Delegates and listened while John Janney, president of the Virginia Convention that had eventually voted for secession, introduced him, announcing his appointment as major general of all land and naval forces in Virginia, echoing the words of Lee's father: "Major General Lee . . . I bid you a cordial welcome to this Hall, in which we may almost hear the echo of the voices of statesmen, the soldiers and sages of bygone days, who have borne your name and whose blood flows in your veins. . . . [Y]ou are at this day, among the living citizens of Virginia, 'first in war.' We pray God fervently that you may so conduct the operations committed to your charge that you are 'first in peace,' and when that time comes you will have earned the still prouder distinction of being 'first in the hearts of your countrymen.'"

Washington's ghost haunted Lee. At Harper's Ferry, among the hostages taken by John Brown and freed by Lee was Lewis W. Washington, George Washington's cousin.

When Lee sent a young officer named James Ewell Brown Stuart (J.E.B. or Jeb Stuart, the future Confederate cavalry commander) to order Brown's surrender, other hostages pleaded that their lives were in danger, but Washington shouted over them: "Never mind us! Fire!"

"The old revolutionary blood does tell," Lee remarked admiringly.

With the outbreak of war, one of Lee's first staff officers was George Washington's nephew, John A. Washington. He was also one of the first casualties, shot down in a Union ambush while riding reconnaissance with Lee's son Rooney in western Virginia.

And it would have been hard, indeed, for Lee not to recognize that he was himself now cast in Washington's role, as the commanding general responsible for ensuring his people's independence. He even wore on his collar three stars of uniform size, as had Washington. In the Confederate army, this designated a colonel. Generals had a larger star in the center, the grouping enveloped by a wreath. But for Lee, the three stars were sufficient—an act of simplicity and of homage to his hero, his countryman, his relation by marriage.

There was a problem, though. Lee had been handed a high responsibility, but the real power lay elsewhere, with the president of the Confederate States of America, Jefferson Davis. The former secretary of war for the United States intended to direct southern military strategy himself from the Confederacy's new capital, Virginia's state capital, Richmond, which was a mere 105 provocative miles from the Federal capital in Washington, D.C.

Unlike many of the officers with whom he would have to deal in these early days of impending war, jockeying for position, fame, and prestige, Lee gave no thought to insubordination, no thought to undermining his commander-in-chief through backroom intrigue designed to advance his own authority. Lee simply expressed his views when asked, but otherwise accepted the president's lead and deferred to him. Rather than seek to expand the powers of his position—or reclaim powers that were rightfully his from the president—Lee focused on the more important task requiring his attention: namely, to raise and outfit a new army for a new nation that awaited imminent invasion.

KNOW YOUR BUSINESS— AND BE DECISIVE

Field Marshall Viscount Wolseley, who ended his career as commander-in-chief of the British army, attested that Lee's creation of the Confederacy's armed forces "was a colossal task. Everything had to be created by this extraordinary man. The South was an agricultural, not a manufacturing, country, and the resources of foreign lands were denied it by the blockade of ports maintained by the fleet of the United States. Lee was a thorough man of business, quick in decision, yet methodical in all he did. He knew what he wanted. He knew what an army should be, and how it should be organized, both in a purely military as well as in an administrative sense."

Lee, creating an army from scratch and in a hurry, was very much in the position of an entrepreneur starting a business—only Lee had to make his business instantly profitable and able to withstand immediate assault from an industrial giant. To accomplish this phenomenal task, Lee exhibited three of his hallmarks of effective leadership.

First, as noted by Viscount Wolseley, Lee "knew what he wanted."

Second, he had a thorough knowledge of his business—he "knew what an army should be."

Third, it was Lee's particular talent, especially in this time of crisis, that he was "quick in decision, yet methodical in all he did."

True to his belief that a good combat officer is first a good administrator, in a mere eight weeks Lee had mobilized an army—with uniforms, equipment, and a command structure. Of the Confederate forces in the field at the battle of First Manassas in July 1861, one-quarter had been raised by Lee. Moreover, he had developed much of the advance strategy that led to Confederate victory in this, the first major engagement of the war.

THE GOOD SUBORDINATE

Lee's work, however, was neither openly heroic nor personally gratifying. The man who hated paperwork was stuck in a desk job. Indeed, he suffered the supreme frustration of having Jefferson Davis keep him in Richmond while the Confederate president himself witnessed the victory of Lee's plans on the battlefield at Manassas.

When he occasionally dispatched Lee to the field, Davis used him as a troubleshooter, though under such ambiguous authority as to make his troubleshooting problematic. He was sent to western Virginia, where the Confederate cause appeared to be foundering. Lee's first assignment there was as an ill-defined consultant to General W. W. Loring, who resented Lee's presence, regarding him as the president's chief emissary for meddling.

Nevertheless, Lee, doing much of the reconnaissance work himself, inspired Loring to take his force—which was demoralized by an outbreak of measles and by rainy, wretched weather—and go on the offensive against the Federals at Cheat Mountain. The operation began well, with the Confederates, despite the dismal weather, successfully finding their assault positions and easily capturing the outlying Federal pickets. But under interrogation, the Federal prisoners convinced Colonel Albert Rust, the officer charged with leading the main assault, that Union strength was much greater than it really was. Rust and his subordinate commanders called off the attack, and Lee was forced to report that his planned offensive had fizzled out into a "forced reconnaissance."

Lee's next experience in western Virginia was no more happy. He was sent to settle the differences between two commanding generals—John B. Floyd and Henry A. Wise, both former Virginia governors—who were mired in jealous rivalry and, even worse, faced potential trouble from the real enemy, the Federals. Lee attempted to unite the generals and lead them in an offensive. But this plan, too, sputtered out in bad weather, bad intelligence, and inaction that allowed the Federal forces to escape.

Lee's assignments in western Virginia were exercises in frustration, where he was forced to act as a diplomat and a consultant with no real authority aside from what the commanding generals chose to give him as President Davis's chief military adviser. But it is to his credit, though little was accomplished—or even could have been accomplished, given the bad weather and the stubborn, petty-minded, politicking generals he had to work with—that Lee at least attempted to take the offensive, to build momentum, to move intransigent officers to act, however poorly, on his plans. He also took the opportunity, when it was later granted him, of transferring every unworthy or incompetent officer he found during this unhappy time in western Virginia out of his army.

Lee was then given command of the South Carolina, Georgia, and eastern Florida coastline, where he shored up coastal defenses. But this was not entirely happy work either. South Carolina was the seat of secession, the home of the fire-breathers, and the lackluster campaigns on which Lee had been an adviser did not endear him to the leaders of the Palmetto State. Relations between Lee and his coastal hosts did not improve when Lee found the defenses such a shambles that he frankly doubted they could be shored up in time to withstand a Federal assault. Lee was also less than impressed by the work ethic and seriousness of the paladins of the Southeastern seaboard. He wrote his daughter Annie, "Our people have not been earnest enough, have thought too much of themselves and their ease, and instead of turning out to a man, have been content to nurse themselves and their dimes, and leave the protection of themselves and families to others."

Worst of all, Lee had to recommend the evacuation of the islands off the Georgia coast and parts of the South Carolina coastline, which the Confederacy simply did not have the resources to defend. Some of the region's wealthiest planters lived there and, as Mary Chestnut observed, "Low-country gentlemen curse Lee." Lee's critics had taken to calling him "Granny Lee" and argued that while he might be a great military theorist, staff officer, and engineer, he was unsuited to actual combat operations.

Davis, to his credit, didn't agree. He had long held Lee in high regard, ever since they were cadets together at West Point, and he perhaps even agreed with General Winfield Scott—who had told President Lincoln that Lee was worth 50,000 men to the South.

Lee was invaluable to Davis, serving as his sounding board, his closest military adviser, and an officer on constant call to discuss strategy. Lee was also a repository for endless work, for whatever Davis couldn't do himself, to ensure that every military department from the commissary to the ordnance operated as it should.

Responsibility did not rest lightly on the shoulders of Jefferson Davis. He worked long hours, drawing departmental charts that provided schematic order to the huge area he had to defend: a coastline that extended from Virginia's Atlantic shores to Texas and the Gulf of Mexico, and a land border that began east of Lee's Arlington home and petered out into the deserts of West Texas. He had to do this with virtually no navy and an army of new recruits against an adversary that outnumbered him nearly four to one in potential combat strength, with nearly four times as much banking capital and nearly 90 percent more manufacturing industry.

After the initial victory at First Manassas, the Southern Confederacy came under swift assault. Confederate forces in western Virginia crumpled, and the territory that would become the state of West Virginia was soon firmly in the hands of the enemy. The South's coast was blockaded, its western armies swept from Kentucky into southern Tennessee. Mississippi had been invaded and New Orleans seized. Fearing the president had more responsibility than he could handle, as battlefield reverses mounted, the Confederate Congress tried unsuccessfully to pressure Davis into delegating authority.

But where the Congress failed, Lee persuaded by building up an enormous reservoir of trust with Davis. Lee's success in eventually being given an increasingly independent field command was due to one of the paradoxes of his lessons on leadership: *a good leader is a good subordinate.*

Lee's service to Davis was in dramatic contrast to that of General Joseph E. Johnston. While Lee served (or languished) at Davis's side and was his troubleshooter on temporary, unrewarding field assignments, Johnston held the field command of Virginia's armies in the front line of the war. While widely considered the Confederacy's most gifted commander at the outset of the war, Johnston was nevertheless not a favorite of Davis. The two had never gotten along, and the prickly general did not improve matters with his complaints over rank and his apparent disregard for the president's advice. Johnston was uncommunicative with the president, believing that dispatches to Richmond only invited Davis or Lee to interfere in his plans, and he found it difficult to accept their authority over him. In one famous instance during the first battle in front of Richmond, the battle of Seven Pines, he actually rode in the opposite direction when Davis appeared on the field.

The fact that Johnston was fighting at Seven Pines was itself a matter of concern. Johnston had retreated to Seven Pines all the way from the Virginia coastline, abandoning, among other things, the city of Norfolk—the center of whatever hopes the Confederacy had of building a navy. Johnston's retreat was, in part, a strategic decision. Johnston was willing, even eager, to go on the offensive, but he believed he needed to concentrate his armies before lashing out, which was basic military doctrine. As such, the strategy had, perhaps, some merit. But Johnston was unwilling to confide in the president, to keep him apprised of his plans, all the while retreating on the capital. Lee, an old friend of Johnston's, had to act as an intermediary so that Davis could be told where— exactly—Johnston intended to stop, if ever, and where he intended to fight.

Some of Johnston's defensive lines were finally drawn within five miles of Richmond's suburbs, within sight of the city's church steeples. A combined Union force of more than 150,000 men now threatened the Confederate capital with attack from both northern and southern approaches. The infant Confederate government secretly planned for a possible evacuation.

In these dire circumstances Lee came to Richmond's rescue: first, by pressing a strategic offensive in another theater, and second, by winning a battlefield promotion—or more accurately, reassignment—that would put him in field command.

From his desk in Richmond, Lee was in communication with General Thomas J. Jackson. Jackson was by all accounts an eccentric, inflexible, and dour Calvinist—a former professor at the Virginia Military Institute, where the cadets called him "Tom Fool" Jackson. But where others saw a strange, unclubbable, rough-hewn man, Lee saw a commander in the Shenandoah Valley who shared his aggressive strategic vision, someone whose confidence in God's will was such as to inspire him to take great risks, someone who—and this was the fundamental point—*understood the revolutionary nature of the struggle.*

Robert E. Lee was a true son of Light Horse Harry. He knew that if the South were to survive as an independent country it could no more rely on conventional military strategy than had the patriots of Lexington and Concord. In "Stonewall" Jackson, he found an officer who responded instinctively to that call.

Lee sent Jackson down the valley—north—to threaten the Potomac. Instead of relying on a concentration of his own forces, Lee worked to avoid a concentration of Union forces by feinting against Washington with Jackson. The strategy worked. The Union army under General Irvin McDowell that was marching to attack Richmond from the north (in conjunction with Union General George McClellan's assault from the south) was halted at Fredericksburg, midway between Washington, D.C., and Richmond. Lee's strategy was as sophisticated as it was aggressive. He showed that *it is more valuable to threaten an opponent where he feels vulnerable than it is to concentrate on the defensive—even when that opponent is manifestly stronger than oneself.* Lee would continue to regard Richmond's defense as imperative— it could not be abandoned—but he also repeatedly denuded it of forces so as to strike the enemy elsewhere, to hit him where he was afraid to be hit, so as to release the pressure on the Confederate capital. As Charles Marshall, an aide to Lee, later recorded: "It was a saying of General Lee that

Richmond was never so safe as when its defenders were absent."

But the full force of Davis's confidence in Lee's daring had not yet come, his battlefield reassignment not yet occurred. Now General Joseph E. Johnston's troops were enshrouded in gunsmoke from the volleys of cannon and musketry that could be heard in Richmond—and *were* heard by Jefferson Davis. The Confederate president rode to the sound of the guns. He found Lee observing the fight, and the two rode together along the front, coming under heavy enemy fire. But worse than the sting of battery smoke was to befall Joseph E. Johnston. He was carried from the field in great pain, barely conscious, badly wounded. Davis turned to Johnston's second-in-command, Gustavus Smith, inquiring about his plans. But Smith was obviously shaken and, with the enemy yet to be driven from the field, unsure what to do. Johnston's wounds and Smith's uncertainty compelled Davis's next fateful decision. With darkness falling, Davis transferred Johnston's field command to Robert E. Lee.

TAKING CHARGE

In contrast to Johnston, Lee, from his very first day as commander in the field, kept up a stream of correspondence to the Confederate president. The tone was deferential, the volume avidly appreciated by the commander-in-chief, who was interested in every detail Lee had to offer. Historian Joseph Harsh says that by "the close of his first week in the field, Lee had established with Davis a working partnership with few parallels in military history and none in the Civil War."

Lee always had Davis's respect, even after he came under criticism for failing to hold western Virginia. But now his openness and honesty, his complete lack of egotism—which highlighted the disinterested clarity of his strategic views—and his deference to Davis as the ultimate deciding authority won the president's complete trust and confidence, and won Lee the independence and delegated authority that others had sought in vain. Colonel Armistead Long, an aide to Lee, noted that Lee "is ever willing to receive suggestions of the President, while the President exhibits the greatest confidence in General Lee's experience and ability, and does not hamper him with executive interference."

Lee was never a political officer, lobbying for preferment. While other officers, like Johnston, jostled over their rank and seniority in the Confederate service, Lee did not. Lee was focused on winning the war, not on advancing his career or jealously guarding his prerogatives. As he had in Mexico, Lee won responsibility through competence. He won field command through that neglected Christian virtue—humility. And here he illustrated another of his paradoxical lessons on leadership: *An effective leader needs to be humble.* Why? Because a leader needs to subordinate himself to his cause, both so that he can envision its goals and its needs clearly, without the gauzy film of ego or self-interest coming in between, and so as to set an example of devotion to duty—a good not only in itself, but to keep one's subordinates focused on the very same goal. As Lee wrote to his daughter-in-law: "I wish that [Johnston's] mantle had fallen upon an abler man, or that I were able to drive our enemies back to their homes. I have no ambition and no desire but the attainment of this object, and therefore only wish for its accomplishment by him that can do it most speedily and thoroughly."

Lee quickly worked to turn his wishes into reality: first, by securing the defenses of Richmond, and second, by taking every available opportunity to drive the Federals back. The first part of this equation, securing Richmond's defenses, was as unpopular with his soldiers as Lee's defensive arrangements along the

South Carolina–Georgia coast had been. The Confederate troops called Lee the "King of Spades" for setting them to digging defensive works. They saw no connection between fighting on the one hand and shifting dirt with a shovel on the other; and, indeed, thought the latter was a weak substitute for the former. In spirit, Lee's men would rather have charged enemy entrenchments than build their own. But Lee was an engineer. In this war, he proved to be an innovator in the use of earthworks, fortifications, and trenches, and also invented railroad-mounted artillery. He used these defensive works not simply to secure a position but to hold that position with fewer men, while Lee moved onto the offensive elsewhere.

Lee knew the work was necessary. But he also knew its necessity was but dimly understood or appreciated by his troops. Still, he was confident that if the work itself achieved the practical goal of improving Richmond's defenses and increasing his men's safety, it would also teach the army a moral lesson. He wrote to President Davis, "Our people are opposed to work. Our troops, officers, community, and press. All ridicule and resist it. It is the very means by which McClellan is advancing. Why should we leave to him the whole advantage of labour? Combined with valor, fortitude, and boldness, of which we have our fair proportion, it should lead to success. What carried the Roman soldiers into all countries but this happy combination. . . . There is nothing so military as labour, and nothing so important to an army as to save the lives of its soldiers."

As Lee noted, the Roman legions built roads and other works. So, later, would the French Foreign Legion. Aside from the military utility of trenches and parapets, Lee knew that the manual labor of field works was a form of physical conditioning for the men. It also imposed discipline and helped rid his army of the tropical indolence he had noted among the defenders of South Carolina and Georgia, which contrasted so dangerously with the Northern troops whom he observed "working like beavers." If Lee practiced an unpopular Yankee frugality in economic manners, so too did he share an unpopular Yankee work ethic.

But his army needed the discipline. Lt. Colonel Robert Chilton described the army Lee inherited as an "armed mob" and a rabble of "undisciplined individuality." It was Lee's task—and his trick—to maintain the army's eager fighting spirit and its capability for initiative while bringing a sense of order and discipline to its conduct and operations. Lee achieved that trick by creating a new army out of the men he inherited. Indeed, he created one of the most famous and effective armies in military history.

Lee's command was inaugurated by his first order, which gave the army a new name that befit his aggressive strategic vision. From now on it was to be known as the Army of *Northern* Virginia. That was where he intended to take the battle. As he wrote to Jefferson Davis, he intended to "change the character of the war." There would be no more retreats in Virginia. From now on, the war would be taken to the enemy. His men knew their task. They retained their individuality, their "Rebel Yell" spirit that told them a single Johnny Reb was worth four Billy Yanks. But they also learned to focus not on many individual goals but on one, on his goal, on their shared goal of liberating their homeland from the Federal invader. One of his cavalrymen—a captain and a future congressman—memorably described the Army of Northern Virginia as a "voluntary association of gentlemen organized for the sole business of driving out Yankees."

Lee was not a distant figure to this "voluntary association of gentlemen." He spent his days riding up and down the lines, encouraging the men in their field work, ordering details to clean up the camps, and making sure that the distribution of food and uniforms was improved. He ended favoritism in an army where many units—catastrophically—elected their own officers, by reorganizing the troops, some of whom had used favorite captains to get themselves assigned to soft duty. He also reorganized the artillery to make it more mobile and effective. And in general he treated the army as though it were—in modern terms—a classic car that needed to be broken down to its component parts, then greased, oiled, refitted, restored, and rebuilt. However anachronistic the metaphor, it fits, because Lee was about to take the army racing.

His subordinate officers, Stonewall Jackson excepted, were at first suspicious of Lee. Many of them had accepted the popular criticisms that Lee was a "paper soldier," a desk-bound officer who was a poor replacement for a tough, old gamecock like Joseph E. Johnston. Their attitudes quickly changed. In his first meeting with his generals, Lee measured their defeatism by asking whether they thought it necessary to retreat closer to Richmond. To his disappointment, they said yes.

But that was not Lee's plan. As Lee told his aide, Colonel Charles Marshall, "If we leave this line because they can shell us, we shall have to leave the next for the same reason, and I don't see how we can stop this side of Richmond." When one of the generals started to draw a diagram to illustrate the necessity of retreat, Lee admonished him: "Stop, stop! If you go on ciphering we are whipped beforehand."

Because he understood the revolutionary nature of the Confederate cause, he knew that textbook strategy had its limits. If the Confederacy was going to win, it had to win against all odds. And if it had to win against all odds, it couldn't play by the odds.

With the entrenchments in front of Richmond completed, Lee defended them with a holding force of 25,000 men, out of a total Confederate strength of roughly 70,000. McClellan faced Richmond with an army of 100,000 men. But using

Richmond as a pivot, Lee hurled his smaller force on an unceasing offensive—like a bulldog taking after a mule, if unable to seize its jugular, then ripping at its hamstrings—in what became known as the Seven Days campaign. The campaign was costly. Not everything went according to plan, and Lee's trust in Stonewall Jackson—whom he had recalled from the Shenandoah Valley to join the campaign—must have been sorely tried, as Jackson, suffering from exhaustion, repeatedly and without apology failed him.

But Lee kept the army surging forward until General McClellan was driven back a full 25 miles, in what McClellan tried to term a strategic withdrawal, but which became known popularly as "the great skedaddle." It would take the Union three years to bring its troops as close to Richmond as they were before Lee took command.

Lee's victory was as symbolic as it was military. The boost to Southern morale and to the morale of his new Army of Northern Virginia was enormous. The victory had its theatrical side, too, with Confederate cavalryman Jeb Stuart's famous ride round McClellan, circumnavigating the Union army, developing intelligence, and taking prisoners. And it was demonstrable in terms of territory and initiative regained. Lee had not only raised the near-siege of Richmond, he had driven the Federals all the way out of Henrico County to Harrison's Landing on the James River.

When Lee took command from Johnston, McClellan had affected to be pleased by the change. "I prefer Lee to Johnston," he said. "The former is too cautious and weak under grave responsibility. Personally brave and energetic to a fault, he is yet wanting in moral firmness when pressed by heavy responsibility, and is likely to be timid and irresolute in action."

But McClellan's dispatches to Washington during the Seven Days soon took on a different tone—one of panic, declaring, "I am in no way responsible . . . I have not failed to represent repeatedly the necessity for reinforcements. . . . If the result . . . is a disaster, the responsibility cannot be thrown on my shoulders." And in another dispatch he wrote, "I have lost this battle because my force was too small. I again repeat that I am not responsible for this. . . . As it is, the Government must not and cannot hold me responsible for the result. . . . [T]he Government has not sustained this army. If you do not do so now the game is lost. If I save this army now, I tell you plainly that I owe no thanks to you or to any other persons in Washington. You have done your best to sacrifice this army."

McClellan's attempt to cover himself politically and deny responsibility for the Federal defeat could not have been more at odds with Lee's firm belief that a commander accepted *every* responsibility. Nor could it be more at odds with Lee's deferential tone in addressing President Davis and his cabinet officers. And nor could it be more different from Lee's manner with those who disappointed him. When Lee came upon Jackson, who had, in his exhaustion, kept his men from executing their key role in Lee's offensive plans and thereby dramatically increased Confederate losses, he merely reined his horse beside him and said dryly, "Ah, General, I am very glad to see you. I had hoped to be with you before." For the dutiful Jackson, it was rebuke enough.

Still, on the defensive, McClellan's troops fought well. So well, indeed, that nearly a third of Lee's available fighting force went down as casualties, compared to 20 percent of the Federals. Lee could not—and *knew* he could not—afford many victories like this. He could not afford the losses and he could not afford the lackluster performance of so many of his subordinate generals. The worst of them would soon be given new assignments. The best of them, though they might have stumbled during the Seven Days, like the hero of the Shenandoah Valley, Stonewall Jackson, and the gallantly impulsive A. P. Hill, would be given a second chance.

Most important of all, Lee knew that the Confederacy could not afford continual retreat and the loss of its capital. Even if it was not, strictly speaking, militarily important to defend Richmond, which was more an albatross than an aid to defending Virginia, even if a better a strategy might have been to fall back on the Blue Ridge Mountains from which, as Lee said, he "could fight those people for years to come," Lee proved that he was no mere military theorist, skilful with paper, pen, and map. He knew the unaffordable political and moral cost that would have been paid by the loss of Richmond. He knew that it was too important for Virginia and for the Confederacy to lose the new nation's capital. Not only must Richmond be defended, but the invader must be driven from her gates. It was Lee's victory to achieve that and to entirely reverse the momentum of the war.

Nevertheless, he was brutally disappointed. Expelling the Federals from Richmond was not the sum of his objectives. His plans were designed to crush McClellan's army, and in his report to Jefferson Davis, Lee stated self-critically, "Under ordinary circumstances, the Federal army should have been destroyed."

But it is a tribute to Lee's achievement that despite the heavy casualties and despite his frustration at not annihilating a force larger than his own, that was better supplied, and that enjoyed an enormous advantage in artillery and near-perfect defensive positions, Lee's men and his officers rallied round their new, aggressive commander. The image of "Granny Lee" was dispelled. The Seven Days campaign began the process of Lee and his Army of Northern Virginia's becoming an inseparable organism of mind and heart. His men respected him as the man who had forced McClellan to turn tail, and Lee respected them for having fought so well and so bravely at such cost. If Lee's critics have faulted him for excessive aggressiveness, it was a trait that his men admired and that suited their own temperament. If the casualty list was high, the men in grey, the men whose lives were actually at risk, preferred not to count the cost but to smile at the retreating bluecoats and take pride in their commander, who had sent them scurrying. As one of Lee's soldiers recalled after long service with Lee:

"Marse Robert" knew . . . that he could trust us to the limits of human endurance. He did not have to ask whether we *would* do a thing. You will not misunderstand when I say that he had only to inquire whether a thing *could* be done— whether it was humanly possible for the numbers he assigned to the task.

If it *could* be done, he knew it *would* be done! Hence the extreme daring of his campaigns. . . .

If he knew he could count on us, we knew we could rely on him, and in our faith in him you have, I think . . . [another] component in the morale of the Army of Northern Virginia. We knew that whatever generalship could accomplish, he would do. We knew he never told us to make a charge unless it had to be made. We knew he never said "hold" unless failure to hold meant disaster to our homes. We were often hungry, but we knew he tried to find us food. We were nearly naked, but we knew he was doing his best to get clothing for us. We were weary oftentimes from the marches he set before us, but were satisfied that he did not call on us to make good his delinquencies. He came daily among us—always the ideal figure of a soldier—and though he never sought popularity by ostentation, when he spoke to us it was with as much affection as of dignity.

For this soldier, Lee's lessons of leadership were twofold: first, a leader must be superlatively competent, and second, he should remember that the most effective leaders, like the Son of Man (to echo the soldier's own King James Bible cadences), come to serve.

Lee's legend was beginning. If his army had absorbed frightful punishment, it had done so like a boxer who has first to fight his way off the ropes before he can take command of the ring. However many body blows McClellan's men had landed on Lee's troops, it was *his* Federal army that was now reeling; the Army of Northern Virginia had its measure.

LEE'S LESSONS

• A good leader is first a good subordinate. Leadership must be earned.

• A leader must be decisive—his decisions a fulfillment of his duty, vision, and experience. "Lee was a thorough man of business, quick to decision, yet methodical in all he did. He knew what he wanted. He knew what an army should be."

• A good leader is humble. He guards against ego distorting his vision. A leader has to achieve his army's or his business's or his team's goals, not his private ones. A leader's role is one of service.

• A leader focuses his subordinates on their common goal and inspires them by his own devotion to achieving it.

• A leader orders hard work and enforces necessary discipline but doesn't suffocate his subordinates' initiative or spirit. His goal is assembling a "voluntary association of gentlemen organized for the sole business" of his enterprise.

◆ A leader needs to understand the nature of his cause. Old rules might not apply. If the odds are against your success, you cannot play the odds and expect to win.

◆ While taking adequate precautions, a leader is aggressive in homing in on his opponent's weaknesses rather than fretting about his own. To reiterate the cliché: The best defense is a good offense. Or in Lee's words: "Richmond is never so safe as when its defenders are absent."

◆ A leader can distinguish between subordinates who make mistakes but have great potential (like Stonewall Jackson) and those who make mistakes and have no potential (and who should therefore be removed).

CHAPTER FIVE

LEE'S WAR

AT THE START of the war, Jefferson Davis had hoped to keep the South's borders inviolate, and he hoped to bring into the Confederacy states that he felt were southern by sentiment, even if Union troops held the upper hand—if not occupied Maryland and Delaware, then at least the border states of Kentucky and Missouri. Confederate armies were even probing into the territories of New Mexico and Arizona.

All this changed, of course, as the Confederacy soon found itself thinking not about expansion but about its very survival. Lee had always taken a more sober estimate of what the War Between the States would mean, and how long it would last. Now in the flush of command, he was no less aware of the difficulties before him. "Conceding to our enemies the superiority claimed by them in numbers, resources, and all the means and appliances for carrying on the war," he wrote, "we have no right to look for exemptions from the military consequences of a vigorous use of these advantages."

Lee's plan was to foil the Union's use of its advantages.

His first task, after driving General McClellan from the outskirts of Richmond, was, as he saw it, to continue his offensive. McClellan's position was virtually impregnable; so

Lee resolved to bring his armies north and push the Union General John Pope out of northern Virginia.

KNOW YOUR ENEMY

Pope's army represented a new threat. First, it sat on the railway lines of Northern Virginia. Second, his was a vast enlargement of the Federal army that, under General Irvin McDowell, had been poised to attack Richmond from the north, but that had been held in place, nervously guarding the approaches to Washington, D.C., by Stonewall Jackson's Valley campaign. Third, Lee saw in Pope a new and ugly face asserting itself in the war. Pope explicitly designated the South's civilian population as a legitimate war target. He gave orders that his army would live off Southern civilians, paying recompense only to those who could prove their loyalty to the Union. All Southern male civilians in territory occupied by Pope were subject to immediate arrest. Both men and women, by his orders, could be executed as spies and traitors for as little as attempting to communicate with family members in the Confederate army.

A war on civilians was not Lee's kind of war. While Lee had perfectly sound strategic reasons for focusing on Pope, there is no denying that he thought Pope offered an example of uncivilized warfare that "ought to be suppressed if possible." Lee, as a defender of Virginia, owed it to his people to draw his sword on the "miscreant Pope."

The task Lee assigned himself, of getting at General Pope and destroying his army, was no easy one. McClellan, on Lee's front, outnumbered the Confederate general even more than he had before the Seven Days. Pope's numbers were also greater than Lee's and would be increased even further if McClellan embarked his troops from the James River and sent them north. Even if McClellan did not concentrate his forces with Pope's, Lee would still have to defend Richmond with one hand and strike Pope with the other.

But if Lee's situation appeared even more perilous, in terms of numbers, than it had before, he was confident that his men, whom he knew better now, were up to the challenge. If the odds on paper were bleak, Lee held to his belief that "If you go on ciphering, we are whipped beforehand." He trusted not to mathematical odds but to his reading his enemy.

It was a good thing he did, because the numbers told a frightening story. Still, Lee divided his forces—"almost disdainfully," in the words of historian William C. Davis—confident that McClellan, the Union's Young Napoleon, would remain at the river.

Lee sent General Jackson and 24,000 men north to harass Pope, who could field an army roughly three times that size. If Pope could be brought to battle or if McClellan's men showed signs of moving north via the James River to assist him, Lee would rush up another 31,000 Confederate forces with General Longstreet.

Lee believed that McClellan would remain as long as possible behind his secure defensive position, where he was open to assault only along a narrow pathway that could be raked by Federal land-based artillery and big guns on U.S. Navy ships anchored in the James River. McClellan might be *ordered* out of his defensive position to combine with Pope, but Lee doubted that either McClellan or his civilian masters in Washington would order a counterthrust at Richmond; the Northern government's fear for the safety of the Federal capital, as Jackson advanced, was simply too great. When Lee received intelligence that McClellan's Federals had been ordered to reinforce Pope, he sped his men north.

TRUST YOUR SUBORDINATES—
AND KEEP THEM AGGRESSIVE

Lee gambled when he gave Stonewall Jackson the lead role in attacking Pope. Jackson had performed brilliantly in the Shenandoah Valley, but sluggishly, at best, under Lee's command in the Seven Days. But Lee believed Jackson would redeem himself, and to assist him in reclaiming his reputation, Lee played to Jackson's strengths. He reminded Jackson, the stern disciplinarian, to guard against stragglers on his rapid march, and he warmed Jackson's offensive spirit by urging him not to *await* opportunities to strike Pope but to *create* them, not to await detailed orders from Lee but to act swiftly and independently within the boundaries of Lee's discretionary orders.

Now on the march, Lee ordered Jackson to bring Pope to battle by putting Jackson's Confederate troopers between Pope's army and Washington. Jackson, who had already clashed with a portion of Pope's army at Cedar Mountain, now maneuvered his army behind Pope's and further annoyed the Union general by burning his supply depot at Manassas Junction. Confederate cavalry commander Jeb Stuart offered his own insult by raiding Pope's camp.

Pope mistakenly thought he had finally "bagged" the slippery Jackson. "I see no possibility of his escape," said Pope. But Jackson was Lee's bramble bush. While Jackson held him, Lee rode up with General Longstreet to hit Pope on the flank, with the intention of sweeping him away as though he were a tumbleweed beside a gate. Pope could put more men on the field than Jackson and Longstreet combined, but Lee knew a leader has to face squarely the necessity of risk, especially when the odds are against him. "The disparity . . . between the contending forces," Lee noted calmly, "rendered the risks unavoidable."

Jackson, generally the hammer rather than the anvil of Lee's army, tenaciously defended his position in what would become the battle of Second Manassas. (It was at First Manassas that he had earned the nickname "Stonewall" for his staunch imperturbability under fire: "There stands Jackson like a stone wall! Rally round the Virginians!") Two of Jackson's best commanders (General William Taliaferro and General Richard Ewell) were down with wounds, and some of his men, their ammunition expended, were now reduced to swinging their muskets as clubs, desperately hurling stones, and lunging with bayonets. Still, Jackson remained steely-eyed and largely unruffled, for he knew that casualties among his officers, with whom he often feuded in any event, were inevitable, and that bayonets were meant to be bloodied. Moreover, the most heavily engaged part of his line was commanded by General A. P. Hill. Personally, the two were antithetical, but in combat, Jackson trusted Hill implicitly, whatever the odds against his fierce division commander.

"Tell him," said Jackson, "if they attack again, he must beat them!"

A staff officer from Hill later reported: "General Hill presents his compliments and says the attack of the enemy has been repulsed."

The grim-visaged Jackson grinned, "Tell him I knew he would do it!"

Hill not only held his line, he joined the counterattack.

When General Longstreet arrived on the flank, he waited, as was his wont, for just the right moment to strike. He kept his full complement of troops drawn up and made a careful survey of the land, unhurried by the obvious pressure on Jackson or by Lee's repeated suggestions that he expedite his assault. Finally, Longstreet smashed the exposed Union line with an artillery barrage that lifted the pressure on Jackson. Then, at Lee's command, Longstreet sent his troops charging into the Federals, rolling the bluecoats up, while Jackson's own troopers jumped over their defensive positions, screaming the Rebel Yell. Under attack from two sides, Pope's army broke into flight—running all the way to Washington, where it met McClellan's tardy relief force.

Lee had again won a victory over forces superior in number and equipment. Jackson's and Longstreet's combined corps totaled 55,000 men. Pope had been reinforced to more than 75,000 men, not counting McClellan's force that was on the march to join him. But, as historian William C. Davis has noted, "Being outnumbered never frightened Lee. Instead, he thought only of the offensive."

As for Pope, even one of his army's own historians had nothing but admiration for Lee's Confederate tigers and harsh words for the Union general who "had been kicked, cuffed, hustled about, knocked down, run over, and trodden upon as rarely happens in the history of war. His communications had been cut; his headquarters pillaged; a corps had marched into his rear, and had encamped at its ease upon the railroad by which he received his supplies; he had been beaten and foiled in every attempt he had made to 'bag' those defiant intruders; and, in the end, he was glad to find a refuge in the intrenchments of Washington, whence he had sallied forth, six weeks before, breathing out threatenings and slaughter."

If Lee achieved all these things, it was in part because he had learned vital lessons from the Seven Days campaign. First, he simplified his plans of attack. In the Seven Days campaign, Lee's plans required complicated maneuvers that his young army was incapable of making without a surfeit of costly errors, delays, and miscommunications. Second, he had learned about his officers, transferred those he found wanting, and consolidated his forces under two corps commanders, Jackson and Longstreet, simplifying his command structure so that, as a believer in delegating authority to his generals in the field, he could feel confident that authority was given to men he could trust. It was partly a measure of their respective performance in the Seven Days campaign, and partly a measure of how Lee intended to use his army, that Longstreet's corps held twenty-eight brigades, while Jackson's had only seven. Jackson's Second Corps was to be Lee's highly mobile "foot cavalry," relentlessly jabbing at the enemy, while Longstreet's First Corps was the bulk of the army, immovable in defense, unstoppable in attack.

If Lee had any misgivings about his victory at Second Manassas, it was that his pursuit of the Union forces was stymied by heavy rain and by the exhaustion of his men, who in all their hard marching had had, in many cases, nothing to eat for three days. Lee's first task would be to find them food, and to do that, his eyes gazed across the Potomac to fields thus far untouched by war.

THE VIRTUES OF AUDACITY

Washington was worried. In the three months since Robert E. Lee had held field command, he had broken the imminent siege of Richmond, ended the Confederate retreat, and driven two Union armies—Pope's and McClellan's—across the Potomac. It was the Federal capital that now feared a siege, that was preparing to evacuate government property to New York, and that was readying clerks for the defense of the city.

Lee's success had liberated not only most of Virginia, but also, indirectly, the North Carolina coastline. In the Old Dominion itself, western Virginia was now under only tenuous occupation, and, in the words of Douglas Southall Freeman, except "for the troops at Norfolk and at Fort Monroe, the only Federals closer than 100 miles to Richmond were prisoners of war and men busily preparing to retreat from the base at Aquia Creek."

Having neatly reversed the situation that confronted Richmond in June, Lee could have staked out a defensive position. But Lee did not intend to let the enemy rest; every victory had to be exploited. Time, Lee felt, was against the Confederacy. Unlike Jefferson Davis, who thought the South could win simply by refusing to surrender, by being as iron-willed as he was himself, by holding on until the North eventually lost its stomach for the war, Lee believed a war of attrition and endurance could only benefit the stronger, better-equipped Federal army and its seemingly illimitable resources. His plan was to take the war to the enemy, to launch an invasion of the North, to shock the government in Washington with the full vigor of Confederate valor, and to crush any Federal army that came out to meet him. Granted, it was a strategy based on enormous risk-taking, but Lee knew that a leader's best alternative is not always the easiest.

Lee summed up the situation, with typical honesty, in a letter to Jefferson Davis: "The army is not properly equipped for an invasion of the enemy's territory. It lacks much of the material of war, is feeble in transportation, the animals being much reduced, and the men are poorly provided with clothes, and in thousands of instances are destitute of shoes. Still we cannot afford to be idle, and though weaker than our opponents in men and military equipments, must endeavor to harass, if we cannot destroy them. I am aware that the movement is attended with much risk, yet I do not consider success impossible, and shall endeavor to guard it from loss."

Remarkable words and a salutary example of true leadership. Lee was never given to rhetorical bombast of the sort that afflicted McClellan and Pope, who could be more belligerent in speech than in battle. Lee gave his superior in Richmond an honest accounting. In his letter, he does not avoid responsibility for the dangers he is about to embrace, but calmly notes that he will attempt the near-impossible—and do so prudentially, guarding against undue loss!

Lee planned an offensive maneuver. He did not intend to lay siege to Washington, but to advance into Maryland—a slave state that harbored Southern sympathizers, a state that had already provided Confederate recruits, a state where his men could find forage unavailable in the devastated wastes of Northern Virginia, and a state to which he might draw the Federal armies away from their defenses in Washington so that they could be defeated in open battle.

There was another factor that Lee considered. It was one thing for the Union to wage war on the South. But if the Confederacy could prove itself formidable enough to fight the Federals on their own ground, might not the voices of peace be strengthened? Might not the North think again about the wisdom—and the cost—of compelling the Southern states to remain in the Union?

After Lee crossed into Maryland, he suggested to President Davis that a formal peace proposal might be made to the Federals, because such "a proposition, coming from us at this time, could in no way be regarded as suing for peace; but, being made when it is in our power to inflict injury upon our adversary, would show conclusively to the world that our sole object is the establishment of our independence and the attainment of an honorable peace."

Though Davis, in the course of events, did not act on Lee's proposal, Lee, as a leader, never lost sight of his war's objective: achieving peace through the North's recognition of an independent South. Lee never let the heat of battle or the pressures of the long and horrible war ignite his temper with thoughts of vengeance or simple destruction, or allow control of the ravenous dogs of war to slip from the leash he kept clenched between his fingers. His war was for Southern freedom, and no other consideration or passion would obscure that single goal.

As the Confederate army marched across the border, Lee issued a proclamation to the people of Maryland, which, while asking for their support, also expressed his characteristic tolerance for freedom of conscience: "No constraint upon your free will is intended; no intimidation will be allowed within the limits of this army, at least. Marylanders shall once more enjoy their ancient freedom of thought and speech. We know of no enemies among you, and will protect all, of every opinion. It is for you to decide your destiny freely and without constraint. This army will respect your choice, whatever it may be; and while the Southern people will rejoice to welcome you to your natural position among them, they will only welcome you when you come of your own free will."

As it turned out, the people of Maryland did not rush to embrace the Confederate cause; they had little to gain by doing so. If they refused to join Lee, they knew that Lee's army would not punish them; after all, Lee had guaranteed the people of this divided state the freedom to choose their loyalty. But if they did rally to Lee's call and Union forces eventually returned to their towns, they knew they would be punished with even tighter restrictions of martial law than had already been imposed in some parts of the state (like the city of Baltimore, where among those jailed as a suspected secessionist was the grandson of Francis Scott Key, author of "The Star Spangled Banner").

Lee understood this calculation and was disappointed but not surprised at the outcome. He remained a realist, not only about the likelihood of Marylanders joining the South but about the prospect of foreign intervention, which excited so many Solons in Richmond. While Lee thought that Southern success on a Northern field might shake the confidence of Northern voters in Lincoln and the Northern war party, he expected no intervention by a new Marquis de Lafayette or a new Baron von Steuben, such as had blessed George Washington in his war for independence, or by the arrival of any other French, German, or British support for the Confederacy.

While it might, initially, appear sensible in terms of realpolitik for the European powers to assist in breaking up the Union, Lee knew that true realpolitik had to compute other factors aside from geopolitical advantage. There was also the issue of domestic sentiment within these countries, and slavery, Lee believed, made the South diplomatically untouchable.

Lincoln would not deliver his Emancipation Proclamation until September 23, 1862, after Lee's invasion of Maryland and after the battle of Sharpsburg (or Antietam, as it is known in the North), and the Proclamation did not become law until January 1, 1863. But Lee knew at the war's outset in 1861 that the North would "be shrewd enough to make the war appear to be merely a struggle on our part for the maintenance of slavery; and we shall thus be without sympathy, and most certainly without material aid from other powers."

In 1864, he reiterated this point to Davis, writing, "As far as I have been able to judge, this war presents to the European world but two aspects. A context in which one side is contending for abstract slavery and the other against it. The existence of vital rights involved does not seem to be understood or appreciated." He concluded with typical realism: "Our safety depends upon ourselves alone."

In 1862, the South's safety depended on Lee taking even greater risks. Having marched his men into enemy-held territory, he again divided his forces. He dispatched the swift-moving Jackson to Harper's Ferry to seize the town and clear it of Federals in order to secure a supply line to the South, while he and Longstreet marched into Union territory.

Despite the ragged state of his army, which made his division of forces even more audacious, Lee was confident. He knew that the best fighters are not necessarily those with the plushest and most comfortable supply depots. The common Southern soldier was generally a poor farmer with no slaves. He fought not for material gain, but for freedom and independence, and to be left alone by the Federal government, whose armies had invaded his homeland. His was the spirit of the old Revolutionary War flag: "Don't Tread on Me." Lee believed it was an unbeatable spirit, and that his people's "old revolutionary blood" would tell again. Here's how one eyewitness Marylander described the invading Army of Northern Virginia:

> I could scarcely believe my eyes; was this body of men moving so smoothly along, with no order, their guns carried in every fashion, no two dressed alike, their officers hardly distinguishable from the privates—were these, I asked in amazement, were these dirty, lank, ugly specimens of humanity, with shocks of hair sticking through holes in their hats, and thick dust on their dirty faces, the men that had coped and countered successfully, and driven back again and again our splendid legions with their fine discipline?
>
> And then, too, I wish you could see how they behaved—a crowd of schoolboys on a holiday don't seem happier. They are on the broad grin all the time. Oh! They are so dirty! ...They were very polite, I must confess. . . . Many of them were bare-footed. Indeed, I felt sorry for the poor misguided wretches, for some were limping along so painfully, trying to keep up with their comrades.

That the Army of Northern Virginia could achieve so much with its soldiers in such a state is a singular reminder that true leadership overcomes—indeed to a certain extent makes irrelevant—material adversity. Despite being one of Lee's great critics, British general and author J. F. C. Fuller noted: "Few generals have been able to animate an army as

[Lee's] self-sacrificing idealism animated the Army of Northern Virginia. . . . What this bootless, ragged, half-starved army accomplished is one of the miracles of history."

Another British officer, Garnet Wolseley, was amused to see that Lee's tent was stamped as "belonging to a colonel of a New Jersey regiment. I remarked upon this to General Lee, who laughingly said, 'Yes, I think you will find that all our tents, guns, and even the men's pouches are similarly marked as having belonged to the United States army.'" When it came to material things, Lee and his men knew how to get by on their own frugal stores—and with the unintended generosity of their adversary.

The fact is, equipment, supplies, uniforms, or the accoutrements of a business, whether they be high-tech office machines, ergodynamic chairs, or beautiful, stain-resistant carpets, are far less important to maintaining morale and achieving success than is simply nurturing devotion to one's cause and keeping one's people focused on securing that objective.

So too with discipline. While Lee had done much to improve the army's discipline—and, in fact, in this very campaign he had ordered shot a soldier who attempted to steal a farmer's pig during battle (General Jackson sent him into the heat of the fighting instead)—the Army of Northern Virginia never lost its sense that individuals mattered, that Lee cared about his men, that they were not an anonymous fighting machine, but individual grey wolves organized into packs for efficiency's sake.

In one of the most charming stories about Lee's leadership, a curious, bearded Confederate once paused to peer into Lee's empty tent. Lee rode up, pulled rein, dismounted, and said to the trooper, "Walk in, Captain. I am glad to see you."

"I ain't no captain, General Lee. I's jest a private in the Ninth Virginia Cavalry."

"Well, come on in, sir. If you aren't a captain, you ought to be."

Lee believed that if a leader was generous with his time, his people would be generous with their effort. He was never too busy to offer his men an encouraging word or to look after their welfare. Nor was he too important to share their privations.

The stories of Lee turning away private offers of food or of easy accommodations are legion, but are perhaps best summarized by this wistful recollection of his aide Walter Taylor:

> His simplicity of taste . . . was especially noticeable in the *ménage* at army headquarters. All the appointments were of the simplest kind. The table furniture was of tin, and while we never really wanted for food . . . we only enjoyed what was allotted to the army generally . . . . General Lee never availed himself of the advantages of his position to obtain dainties for his table or any personal comfort for himself. The use of spirituous liquors, while not forbidden, was never habitual in our camp. There was no general mess-supply and rarely, if ever, a private nip. I used to think that General Lee would have been better off if he had taken a little stimulant.

Maryland was not meant to be the end of Lee's campaign. He would, according to his plan, ride into Pennsylvania and strike its railroad at Harrisburg, both to disrupt Federal troop movements, and to threaten three major northern cities—Philadelphia, Baltimore, and Washington, in a descending arc. He meant not only to change the complexion of the war but possibly even to end it. This was an election year, and if Lee could bring Confederate troops to Maryland and Pennsylvania, perhaps Northern voters would be inclined to cut hostilities short, lift the danger to their own security, and return a congressional majority in favor of peace.

But then, something went wrong.

In one of the great turning points of the war, Union troops found three cigars wrapped in a sheet of paper. The paper was a duplicate of Lee's Special Orders No. 191 belonging to one of General D. H. Hill's staff officers—no one knows which one. The orders were delivered to McClellan, who now knew Lee's entire plan of maneuver and knew how dangerously divided Lee's forces were. Lee, who trusted his ability to read McClellan, was surprised to receive intelligence reports that showed the Union general moving with uncharacteristic rapidity toward Lee's vulnerable army, as though he knew its exact location and where it was heading—which of course he did.

Lee's Army of Northern Virginia had gone from the supreme triumph of leading a Northern invasion to the supreme hazard of facing a force more than twice as large, that was privy to Lee's plans, and that could conceivably shut off his line of retreat. Even this description does not convey the full force of Lee's danger. McClellan was bringing 75,000 men to the attack. Lee's full strength was only 38,000 men, and he could bring that number to the field only if Jackson's corps returned in time from Harper's Ferry.

If Lee had hoped his audacity could win the war, now McClellan was convinced that his interception of Lee's plans meant that crushing victory would be his. "Here is a paper with which if I cannot whip Bobby Lee I will be willing to go home."

Lee dispatched roughly 15,000 men to impede McClellan's advance through a gap in Maryland's Catoctin Mountains, while he considered the possibility of retreat. With Jackson at Harper's Ferry, Lee would be outnumbered four to one if he had to fight McClellan now, and at a minimum he had to concede that his ambitious plans to march into Pennsylvania were over.

Lee decided to pull back to the Maryland town of Sharps-burg on Antietam Creek. As he received word that Jackson would soon complete the capture of Harper's Ferry, Lee decided to make a stand. He would not let McClellan chase him out of Maryland. McClellan would have to fight him.

The odds against Lee changed with the clock, each advancing hour bringing him a greater surety. As Lee arranged his men at Sharpsburg, he brought barely a quarter as many troops as McClellan to the field. By afternoon, with the arrival of Jackson, he had shaved the odds to three to one. And at full strength, which he did not have until the battle was nearly over, he was still outnumbered by two to one.

The battle was desperate. In the first four hours of combat, 13,000 men in blue and grey fell as casualties in the bloodiest day of the war.

At one point in the heat and smoke of battle, there was a poignant moment for Lee. An artillery commander reported that a battery had lost three out of four cannons, their crews and their horses dead. Lee ordered the remaining piece back into the action. One of its gunners was a begrimed slip of a man who came forward to pay his respects. It was Lee's youngest son, Rob.

"General," he asked, "are you going to send us in again?"

Lee smiled and replied, "Yes, my son. You all must do what you can to help drive these people back."

Twice, the Confederate line was almost overwhelmed: first at Bloody Lane, where the Confederates, mistakenly thinking they had been ordered to retreat, nearly allowed their forces to be divided; and then late in the day when Lee's right flank, which he had continually stripped to support his left, began to give way under a fierce, sustained attack by Union General Ambrose Burnside. As the flank finally dissolved under Federal fire, Burnside had a clear field to destroy Lee's army.

Lee, who had been confident in the morning and unruffled throughout, now pointed to the southwest, asking an artillery lieutenant to use his field glasses and identify a new unit marching toward the battle. Were they yet more Union troops? The lieutenant saw the snap of Virginia and Confederate flags, though many of the men appeared to be dressed in blue.

Lee knew who it was immediately: "A. P. Hill from Harper's Ferry." Their uniforms were a way to make do, replacing their own tatterdemalion grey with confiscated Federal stores.

Confederate General A. P. Hill, who had been left to finish the job at Harper's Ferry, had started his men as soon as he could, leading them on a 17-mile forced march. Of the 5,000 who started that morning, only 3,000 remained, the others having fallen out or been left straggling behind. With serendipitous precision, Hill arrived exactly when and where the Confederates needed him most, on Burnside's flank. Despite the rigors of his march, Hill's men tore into the Federals, scattering the Union assault. The day was over. But the danger, of course, was not.

Lee could have skedaddled, as McClellan had done before Richmond. But he ordered no retreat. His men made camp and rested. The next day, when the sun rose over a grim battlefield littered with grotesque rows of swollen corpses, Lee's army was still in place, bloody but unshaken, daring McClellan to attack.

McClellan declined the opportunity, content to watch Lee's army from afar. Indeed, McClellan feared that without reinforcements, his own army, more than twice the size of Lee's, shod where Lee's army was not, well-fed where Lee's army was not, and with an endless supply of arms, ammunition, and other supplies that Lee's army had to conserve, was actually in danger of destruction. McClellan would later report that "at that moment—Virginia lost, Washington menaced, Maryland invaded—the national cause could afford no risks of defeat."

Can there be any greater testimonial to Lee's success in shaping and leading the Army of Northern Virginia—and of the virtue of his aggressive strategy—than this timorous assessment from McClellan?

If Lee had come to the brink of disaster, he remained calm and confident—and with good reason. While the engagement at Sharpsburg had blunted his invasion—indeed, effectively ended it—the Army of Northern Virginia had not only survived but achieved what amounted to a brilliant tactical victory. It had held its ground against overwhelming odds, and held it again without challenge the next day. Lee, notes military historian Lt. Colonel Joseph Mitchell, "knew his soldiers as no other man ever did. He was determined that the Army of Northern Virginia was not to believe that it had ever been driven from any field. It was not then, and it never was." Its honor assured, that night Lee pulled the men out of their lines and led them back across the Potomac to the safety of Virginia, with A. P. Hill smacking a contingent of pursuing Federals into the north bank of the Potomac and providing, in the words of Shelby Foote, "a sort of upbeat coda, after the crash and thunder of what had gone before."

Lee's men were rested, refitted, and fed, while Jeb Stuart raised Southern morale—and increased McClellan's caution—by leading his cavalry in another ride around the Army of the Potomac, taking the Confederate horsemen as far north as Chambersburg, Pennsylvania. Then came more interesting news: President Lincoln had relieved General McClellan from command. Lee greeted the announcement humorously, saying of McClellan, "we always understood each other so well. I fear they may continue to make these changes till they find someone whom I don't understand."

Lee would soon be facing a new threat, as a frustrated President Lincoln and his Secretary of War Edwin Stanton took a more active role in directing Union strategy. With General Ambrose Burnside, they plotted a straight course from Washington to Fredericksburg to Richmond. The only thing that stood in their way was the army of General Robert E. Lee.

LEE'S LESSONS

• A leader has the integrity to face facts—and the courage not to be intimidated by them.

• A leader is strategically and tactically aggressive: make the most of opportunities, constantly advance toward your objective. "We cannot afford to be idle."

• A leader does not expect the intervention of others to save himself or his plans. He knows that "Our safety depends on ourselves alone."

• A leader keeps his people focused on their common objective; morale is the product of a leader's vision and example.

• A leader knows that if he is generous with his time, his people will be generous with their efforts.

• A leader keeps his strategic plans simple, and his chain of command streamlined.

• An effective leader knows the mind of his opponent, and knows what his own people can achieve.

CHAPTER SIX

THE HIGH TIDE OF LEE'S CONFEDERACY

LEE DID NOT want to fight at Fredericksburg. It was then only a small city, but for the people who lived there, the hardship of facing a Federal invasion was no less severe. It was a hardship Lee would rather have spared them, particularly as the city was noted more for its charm and its history than for any militarily useful industry. Lee told the Federals that he would consent not to occupy the city, if they would do the same. But the Union's objectives, as we have seen, were to wage war on the people of the South so as to bend them to the Union's will. So, in bitter cold, the women of Fredericksburg, their children, and the men too old to fight gathered their belongings and trudged through the deep snow, evacuating their homes, which the Federals had threatened to shell. As the civilians marched from the looming battlefield, they were pelted by sleet.

Lee looked on the spectacle with wonder, sorrow, and admiration. The townspeople, he noted, "cheerfully incurred great hardships and privations, and surrendered their homes and property to destruction rather than yield them to the hands of the enemies of their country."

Lee preferred to keep fighting away from civilians. But when the Federals chose the route of attack, he was given little choice but to meet them here.

Fighting at Fredericksburg displeased Lee for another reason. While the ground to the west of the city was easily defensible, it was not ground from which he could maneuver. The Federals, if beaten, would simply return across the Rappahannock and have an easy line of retreat to Washington.

Lee and Jackson were not defensive soldiers. They shared a liking for battlefields where success could be followed by success, where one victory led to the possibility of successive victories, where offensive maneuvering offered a continually changing array of prizes to be plucked, situations to be exploited. At Fredericksburg, however, Lee might repel an attack, but do little more.

Lee prepared defensive positions for his army on the hills to the west of the city, in a seven-mile line facing the Rappahannock River, carefully positioning his artillery for maximum effect. Unlike his defense of Richmond, Lee did not set his men to digging trenchworks, relying instead on the natural terrain that gave him the high ground. He knew his defensive position was strong. He wanted to ensure that Burnside would attack. Lee's objectives were plain: "I shall try to do them all the damage in our power when they move forward."

Lee's initial line of resistance was a deployment of Mississippi riflemen who sniped at the Federals as they first bombarded Fredericksburg, then crossed the river and advanced into the city. During the Federal artillery assault on the homes of those whom Lee had seen evacuated, he expressed his disgust at the destruction. He knew Fredericksburg's history. He knew that in that picturesque little city was the former law office of James Monroe, the boyhood home of John Paul Jones, and the former home of George Washington's mother Mary,

Lee's own grandmother-in-law. "Those people delight to destroy the weak and those who can make no defense," Lee growled. "It just suits them."

Lee's Mississippians, under the command of General William Barksdale, whose streaming white hair was as long as a Cherokee's, were gallant in slowing the Union advance, but by evening the Mississippians were withdrawn—very much against their will; some even had to be put under arrest to force them to cease firing. The Federals were uncontested occupiers of Fredericksburg, at least for the moment.

The Union troops busied themselves looting the houses—not just stealing but destroying. Like Cromwell's army smashing papist icons, the Union troops slashed paintings, crashed rifle butts into cabinets and mirrors, and carved, cut, and defaced the belongings of the evacuated civilians. But they would receive a terrible punishment the next day.

The morning opened with fog so thick that cavalry commander Jeb Stuart and an aggressive Stonewall Jackson thought the Confederates should launch a surprise attack under its cover. Lee demurred. He knew there were times when one should accept the advantage of a defensive position. This was one of them. However aggressive Lee's own inclinations, his paramount consideration was always the same: *Make the best of the circumstances in which you are placed.* Often, especially in the battles that would follow, that meant—as Stuart and Jackson advised—seizing the initiative with unexpected offensives. But one of the tests of leadership is weighing the options offered by circumstances and choosing the right one. At Fredericksburg, Lee's defensive position was perfect. He knew it, and he knew an offensive maneuver here would throw away all his natural advantages. By holding firm, he was about to deliver the Federals a shocking blow.

Union guns belched smoke and thunder, trying, largely unsuccessfully, to find the Confederates. As the fog slowly lifted, the artillery battle become a duel—a duel between an entire line of Union cannon and a single Confederate artillery officer with two guns, one of which was quickly disabled. From his position on what became known as Lee's Hill, General Lee saw Captain John Pelham fight 16 Union guns with but one of his own. "It is glorious to see such courage in one so young," Lee said. But even for Pelham's swashbuckling commander, Jeb Stuart, the odds were starting to look a little foolhardy. Stuart sent orders for Pelham to retire. But like the Mississippi sharpshooters before him, Pelham had to be compelled, with three sets of orders, before he would withdraw his cannon and pull back from the fight.

The Federal artillery barrage intensified. Then the Federal infantry began testing the Confederate line, advancing uphill in force. The Confederates waited until the Union soldiers were well in the open before unleashing a deadly artillery barrage of their own. The Federals fell back, only to come again at the Confederate line. It would be a day of slaughter, with the Federals repulsed, once, twice. . . .

It was here, on a hill overlooking the battle, that Lee uttered one of his most memorable phrases—indeed, one of the most memorable phrases in the history of war. "It is well that war is so terrible," Lee said. "We should grow too fond of it."

While Jackson had some hard fighting on Lee's right, Burnside massed the bulk of his forces for an almost obsessive assault on Lee's left at Marye's Heights. Lee saw the Federals were taking a horrible beating, but warned Longstreet that the Union concentration was so heavy that it might break through. The Federal strength was 120,000 men to 78,000 men for the Confederates. But Longstreet, who preferred to fight on the defensive, was phlegmatic: "General, if you put every man now on the other side of the Potomac on that field to approach me over the same line, and give me plenty of ammunition, I will kill them all before they reach my line." The Union soldiers came on, and were shot down, all day.

As night fell, Lee finally ordered his men to dig in. Burnside, he concluded, would come again. Lee was right about Burnside's intention but wrong about his resolution. Burnside's subordinate officers talked him out of renewing the battle; they had had enough of futile slaughter. As Lee wrote his wife, "This morning they were all safe on the north side of the Rappahannock. They went as they came, in the night. They suffered heavily as far as the battle went, but it did not go far enough to satisfy me. . . . The contest will have to be renewed." Lee was disappointed, because a failure to destroy Burnside's army here and now meant more fighting later.

In a Christmas letter to his wife, less than two weeks after the battle, Lee reflected on all that he had seen at Fredericksburg—the civilians displaced, their homes destroyed, and the foe that had slipped away—and he wrote:

But what a cruel thing is war. To separate and destroy families and friends and mar the purest joys and happiness God has granted us in this world. To fill our hearts with hatred instead of love for our neighbors and to devastate the fair face of this beautiful world. I pray that on this day when "peace and good will" are preached to all mankind, that better thoughts will fill the hearts of our enemies and turn them to peace. . . . Our army was never in such good health and condition since I have been attached to it and I believe they share with me my disappointment that the enemy did not renew the combat of the 13th. I was holding back all that day, and husbanding our strength and ammunition for the great struggle for which I thought he was preparing. Had I divined that was to have been his only effort, he would have had more of it. But I am content. We might have gained more but we would have lost more and perhaps our relative condition would not have been improved.

Lee might not have won the complete destruction of Burnside for which he had hoped, but he did succeed in ending Burnside's command of the Army of the Potomac. A month after the battle, and only days after he had tried, and failed, to retake the offensive in what became known as "the Mud March," Burnside offered to resign. He was transferred to Ohio, and the coarse, brash Joseph Hooker took his place. May "God have mercy on Bobby Lee," Hooker said, "for I shall have none."

CHANCELLORSVILLE

Joseph Hooker brought the largest-yet Army of the Potomac into the field to put an end to the career of Robert E. Lee. The Federals had 134,000 men under arms against only 60,000 Confederates, with one of Lee's best divisions, General John Bell Hood's, and one of his corps commanders, General Longstreet, reassigned to the defense of Virginia's southern coast.

Hooker's plan was to advance on Fredericksburg and then divide his army, taking the larger portion on a flanking movement to Lee's rear while the smaller portion advanced from Fredericksburg to the west. Lee, under Hooker's plan, would be crunched in a Union vise.

Most generals facing the prospect of being attacked on two sides—and outnumbered on both—would undoubtedly beat a hasty retreat out of harm's way. But not Lee. He detached a small force of about 10,000 men to hold the roughly 23,000 Federals at Fredericksburg, and turned his attention to confronting Hooker's main force of more than 73,000 men that was coming round behind him. To Hooker's amazement, Confederate General Stonewall Jackson launched an immediate attack on the Federal line. Hooker was so stunned by the Confederates' audacity that he actually ordered his much larger army to retreat, requested reinforcements from Fredericksburg, and began building defensive entrenchments. But Hooker didn't retreat far enough.

That night Lee mused, as he often did, on the question, "How can we get at those people?" It wasn't an abstract thought he kept to himself. Lee believed in consulting with his generals, talking through alternative approaches, finding their weak points, and explaining his own views and objectives so that they were thoroughly understood. In the process, he educated his commanders.

Lee's objective at Chancellorsville was a typically daring one. Though outnumbered, Lee wanted to take the battle to Hooker, and wanted Jackson to lead an attack on the Federal flank. The question was how the Confederates could get around the Union defenses.

After scouting the Union position, Jackson proposed dividing the Confederate army even further. Lee would retain 17,000 men (and be outnumbered four to one against Hooker's entrenched forces), while Jackson took 26,000 men on a bold flanking movement across the Federal front, shielded by forest, to strike the Federal right. "This," in the words of Lee biographer Emory Thomas, "was audacity to the point of madness."

The conversation between the two generals has been recorded as going something like this:

"General Jackson, what do you propose to do?"

"Go around here."

"What do you propose to make this movement with?"

"With my whole corps."

"What will you leave me?"

"The divisions of Anderson and McLaws."

"Well, go on."

Here we see Lee's supreme self-confidence as a leader, unafraid of embracing the most audacious plans of his subordinates—plans that put himself at direct risk—trusting his men and sure they share his vision. If Jackson's plan was madness, it was a madness Lee shared, a madness to "get at those people," to continually find ways to bring them to battle so that they could be crushed. Lee's very desire—which was constant—to bring his outnumbered army to grips with the Federals is the most profound expression of Lee's confidence in his men, which was returned a thousandfold, and his faith both that they could perform phenomenal feats of battlefield valor and that Providence would turn all things to right.

As for his audacious lieutenant in particular, Lee trusted Jackson, because Jackson shaped a plan of action that suited Lee's own aggressive thinking. As Lee later said of Jackson: "Such an executive officer the sun never shone on. I have but to show him my design, and I know that if it can be done it will be done. No need for me to send or to watch for him. Straight as the needle to the pole he advances to the execution of my purpose." For those who seek to follow in Lee's executive footsteps the lesson is clear: *Find your Stonewall.* Find subordinate officers you trust and who share your vision, and turn them loose.

Lee knew that megalomania, egotism, executive interference, and micromanagement are horrible impediments to effective leadership—that they cause more problems than they could ever possibly cure, that they demoralize subordinates and make them timid, and that they are based on the terrible fallacy that one central authority, with inevitably imperfect knowledge, should overrule officers in the field who are better acquainted with the actual detail of the battle. Lee's leadership style is the combat corollary of Friedrich von Hayek's classic defense of the free market in his famous book *The Road to Serfdom,* which shows that command economies—whether fascist, communist, or socialist—are in every way inferior to free-market economies, where decision making is delegated down to countless individuals freely responding to a wealth of diverse economic information and demands.

If a business leader wants to inspire entrepreneurship among his subordinates, he should follow Lee's example. For Lee wanted to see initiative among junior officers, and wanted to do nothing to inhibit it. In this, Lee was guided not only by his own love of liberty—"I am fond of independence"—but by the South's individualistic traditions. An overly restrictive command structure was something Southerners could not abide. More than that, it was something Lee could not afford.

Especially given the odds against him, Lee recognized that his junior officers had to seize every advantage they could gain on the field. He did not want them continually looking to him for advice—by which time an opportunity might have been lost. He saw his role as developing a plan, providing discretionary orders for the execution of that plan, and then leaving the execution to his officers in the field. He wanted them to be aggressive, to be free to take advantage of the inevitable unforeseen opportunities of battle. He knew that—contrary to the impulse of a micromanager—*the greater the risk, the more one must rely on trust.* Hence Lee could say calmly, "Well, go on."

By way of contrast, try to imagine how Union generals McClellan or Hooker or Pope or Burnside would have acted if they were in Lee's place, outnumbered on two sides. The contrast could not be more striking. The Army of the Potomac feared risk-taking even with the benefit of *superior* numbers. McClellan, Pope, Burnside, and Hooker would all have fled to Washington. These generals would never have dreamed of attacking and would have regarded as mad any subordinate who proposed what Stonewall Jackson did. McClellan, Pope, Burnside, and Hooker didn't trust their subordinates the way Lee did, nor were they willing to face Lincoln's wrath if such a wild gamble failed.

Not only would these Union generals have rushed their troops to safety, they would have bombarded President Lincoln with reports of the dreadful odds against them, begged for obviously needed reinforcements, boasted of the great victory they had achieved in pulling the Union army from the jaws of death, and waited on the north side of the Potomac until they had amassed a gargantuan, finely trained, and lavishly supplied army before crossing again into Virginia. And in all these things, they might very well have been right.

But Lee's report to President Davis about the impending attack was, if anything, low-key to the point of madness, noting little more than that "the enemy is in a strong position at Chancellorsville and in large force. . . . I am now swinging around to my left to come behind him." He then went on to comment on operations in western Virginia.

Lee's understatement was natural, but the facts were stark. On his "swinging around to my left" hung the fate of the Army of Northern Virginia, and, by that measure, the fate of the Confederacy.

Hooker, meanwhile, admired the impressive fortifications his troops had built and watched his own troop strength grow. He expected to take advantage of Lee's aggressiveness. He imagined Lee vainly assaulting his immovable line, after which Hooker would chase the shattered, bleeding Confederates into anemic retreat, catching them—even weaker now—in the pincer movement he had planned originally.

But Hooker's dream was mere fantasy. While he rubbed his hands in eager expectation of Confederate self-destruction, a ragged army in butternut and grey was marching hard in a long arcing movement, racing against the fading day. Near dusk, at 5:15 P.M., General Jackson gave the order.

"Are you ready, General Rodes?" Jackson asked.

"Yes sir."

"You can move forward then."

Yankee troops were jolted from their campfires by a terrifying scream—the Rebel Yell—as the sweating, hard-marched Confederates broke into a run, crashing through the woods. The bluecoats scattered in fear, dropping packs, rifles, fleeing with horror-stricken eyes, as the Confederates rolled over the line, hooting, hollering, firing, bayonets lunging forward.

"They are running too fast for us," one Confederate officer remarked to Jackson. "We can't keep up with them."

"They never run too fast for me, sir. Press them, press them!"

The one enemy the Confederates could not beat was time. As darkness fell onto the field, so did confusion. Jackson, however, knew that if Confederate units were disordered, the Federals were in complete chaos, and he was eager to give the Union troops no respite, no chance to reform and turn their superiority in numbers against him. He intended to press his attack through the night.

Scouting ahead of his own lines to see how he could capitalize on his smashing success, Jackson was shot by Confederate fire that mistook him and his staff officers for a Federal patrol. Jackson was badly wounded, but no one yet knew that his wounds would prove mortal.

During the next day's fighting, Hooker was nearly as incapacitated as Jackson. A cannon ball struck the porch on which Hooker was standing, and a splintered beam hit his head, leaving him dazed all day, a condition not improved by his ordering himself a supply of medicinal brandy. (Hooker, a heavy drinker, had foresworn alcohol for the duration of the campaign, until this conk on the head.)

When Lee was informed of Jackson's wounds, he replied, "Ah, Captain, any victory is dearly bought which deprives us of the services of General Jackson, even for a short time." But he chose not to let his mind dwell on it. "Don't talk about it," he told a junior officer. "Thank God it is no worse." And again: "I know all about it and do not wish to hear any more—it is too painful a subject."

Lee was always able to focus his attention on what he could do to improve a situation. That was his role as a leader. There was nothing he could do for Jackson personally, but he could still try to make the most of Jackson's victory, and it was to that end that he devoted his energies.

Command of the attacking Confederate forces had fallen to Jeb Stuart. Lee admonished him to carry on in the spirit of Jackson. "Those people must be pressed today," he wrote. "It is necessary that the glorious victory thus far achieved be prosecuted with the utmost vigor, and the enemy given no time to rally."

Hooker's forces continued to fall back from Chancellorsville, but the Federal troops on Lee's other front were shoving hard against Confederate General Jubal A. Early's skeleton defense outside Fredericksburg. Lee reinforced Early with two more divisions who shifted the tide, driving the Federals back across the Rappahannock River. With that Federal threat cleared away, Lee looked to renew his offensive against Hooker, only to find that the Union commander had also sought the safety of the north bank of the river. As one Union officer confessed: "They have beaten us fairly; beaten us all to pieces; beaten us so easily." In New York, in the newspaper offices of Horace Greeley, the reaction was worse: "My God, it is horrible—horrible! And to think of it—130,000 magnificent soldiers so cut to pieces by less than 60,000 half-starved ragamuffins!"

On May 3, when victory was assured but the battle not yet over, Lee rode to Chancellorsville's front lines.

The scene is one that can never be effaced from the minds of those who witnessed it. The troops were pressing forward with all the ardour and enthusiasm of combat. The white smoke of musketry fringed the front of the line of battle, while the artillery on the hills in the rear of the infantry shook the earth with its thunder, and filled the air with the wild shrieks of shells that plunged into the mass of the retreating foe. To add greater horror and sublimity to the scene, Chancellor House and the woods surrounding it were wrapped in flames. In the midst of this awful scene, General Lee . . . rode to the front of his advancing battalions.

Lee's aide Charles Marshall continues, describing Lee's effect on the men, as his appearance sparked

. . . one of those uncontrollable outbursts of enthusiasm which none can appreciate who have not witnessed them. The fierce soldiers, with their faces blackened with the smoke of battle, the wounded, crawling with feeble limbs from . . . the devouring flames, all seemed possessed with a common impulse. One long, unbroken cheer . . . rose high above the roar of battle, and hailed the presence of the victorious chief. He sat in the full realization of all that soldiers dream of—triumph; and as I looked upon him in the complete fruition of the success . . . I thought that it must have been from such a scene that men in ancient days rose to the dignity of gods.

And at this supreme moment of triumph, what did the glittering general of the Confederacy most desire? "All that I want them to do," he confessed, speaking of the Federal invader, "is to leave us what we are, plain Virginia farmers."

Chancellorsville was the greatest Confederate victory of the war, won against the longest odds, but for which the Confederates paid an enormous price in the death of Stonewall Jackson.

War, as Confederate General Nathan Bedford Forrest famously said, "means fighting and fighting means killing," but the horrible butcher's bill of war did not blind Lee to the fact that men are not replaceable. Not only could the South not replace its grievous losses in manpower, but the genius of individual officers once lost could not be restored. *People matter, individuals matter; no system, however well-oiled, and no leader, however omnicompetent, can afford to ignore the importance of personnel.*

Lee, as Vice Admiral James Stockdale has noted, was a "person" man. When surveying his troops on the battlefield, he never used a unit's number, he wanted to know the colonel's name who commanded. He made his troop dispositions not in accordance merely with the dictates of terrain or textbook strategy, but on the basis of the character of the individual officers. Stonewall Jackson was Lee's strike force—as at Chancellorsville. James Longstreet was Lee's immovable defender—as at Marye's Heights in Fredericksburg. John Bell Hood's Texans were Lee's beloved shock troops who could jar open any Union line, or countercharge and bring to a shuddering halt any Union advance. In this, as in so much else, Lee's mind was opposed to theoretical abstraction and wedded to the reality that individuals are different. He knew that understanding individuals' different qualities is crucial to making the most of their talents to achieve one's ultimate aim. While organizational systems are important, it is the individual officers in charge, and those who serve under them, who really matter. As the war progressed and casualties mounted, it was the growing shortage of truly exceptional officers that most worried Lee.

But of all Lee's losses, Jackson's was the worst. Lee wrote to his wounded general, "Could I have directed events, I would have chosen for the good of the country to be disabled in your stead." To one of the army's chaplains, Lee noted that Jackson's arm had been amputated. "He has lost his left arm, but I have lost my right." Pneumonia was to claim Jackson's last breath. The "great and good" Jackson was gone, and with him, perhaps, went the cause of the Confederacy. His loss would be felt immediately, on the next great campaign.

LEE'S LESSONS

✦ A leader's one unalterable rule: assess circumstances and make the best of them.

✦ A leader consults his subordinates. Talk through alternative approaches and explain your views. It is the best teaching tool you have.

✦ Learn to delegate. Find your Stonewall, find subordinate officers you trust and who share your vision, and turn them loose.

✦ The best motivator—as with Jackson—is to grant your officers independence and responsibility.

✦ The greater the risks, the more a leader must trust his subordinates.

✦ Keep your composure. A leader should take great risks and bear terrible strife with equal equanimity. A leader should never submit his judgment to emotional swings.

✦ People matter, individuals matter; no system, however well-oiled, and no leader, however omnicompetent, can afford to ignore the importance of personnel and having the right people in the right posts.

CHAPTER SEVEN

GETTYSBURG

ANOTHER ONE WAS GONE. On June 28, 1863, General Joseph Hooker joined the ranks of the defeated—McClellan, Pope, and Burnside—and resigned command of the Army of the Potomac, to be replaced by General George A. Meade.

Meade had little time to draw up grand plans for his own great offensive, because Lee's army was already coming at him. Lee had launched his second invasion of the North.

Lee's strategy was similar to his previous invasion of Maryland, which had resulted in the battle of Sharpsburg the year before. He needed to bring relief to Virginia, to lift the Union's devastation of her farmland. He needed to feed his troops, and there was little food to be had in the war-torn Old Dominion. And finally, as always, he wanted to get at the enemy and defeat him whole. He did not want a situation where the Federals would have their noses bloodied and then retreat to safety. He wanted to maneuver the Army of the Potomac into the field so that he could land it a devastating knockout blow, complete its destruction, and give the peace party in the North a signal case to point to, illustrating the futility of the Union's war, and urging an end to hostilities.

There were fire-breathing voices in the South who, encouraged by Lee's victories, spurned any talk of peace. Peace talks, they held, would be a sign of weakness. Worse, they would force the South to consider the prospect of peace with reunion, which was heresy. Southern valor alone would hammer the North into accepting Southern independence. Lee was more realistic. Jefferson Davis, he knew, sympathized with the fire-breathers. Nevertheless, Lee saw wisdom in pursuing peace not only through battlefield victories but through direct nego-tiation. He wrote President Davis that if the people of the North could be convinced that immediate peace might bring eventual reunion, "the war would no longer be supported [in the North], and that, after all, is what we are interested in bringing about." There "will be time enough to discuss its terms," he wrote, "and it is not the better part of prudence to spurn the proposition" beforehand.

While Lee's armies advanced, he wanted a diplomatic ad-vance as well—an advance on all fronts. He wouldn't get it. While he could advise the president, he could control only the Army of Northern Virginia. One of his first acts after Chan-cellorsville was to reorganize it.

Lee's confidence in his army was supreme. He wrote Gen-eral Hood, "Our army would be invincible if it could be properly organized and officered. There never were such men in an army before. They will go anywhere and do anything if properly led. But there is the difficulty—proper comman-ders—where can they be obtained? But they are improving—constantly improving. Rome was not built in a day, nor can we expect miracles in our favor."

Many of Lee's officers were—naturally enough, given the revolutionary situation into which they were plunged—civil-ians who had flocked to the colors. Lee admired their spirit and knew that some of them were extremely gifted amateurs. Cavalry commander Wade Hampton, for example, was one of the wealthiest planters in the South and was in the aristo-cratic tradition of landowners who felt—and often proved—

that they were born to lead in any situation. But as a rule, Lee showed a preference for appointing professionals to his key posts.

Lee wrote Jefferson Davis of his plans: "I have for the past year felt the corps of this army were too large for one commander. Each corps contains when in fighting condition about 30,000 men. These are more than one man can properly handle and keep under his eye in battle. . . . They are always beyond the range of his vision and frequently beyond his reach. The loss of Jackson from command of one half the army seems to me a good opportunity to remedy this evil."

For Lee, as for any effective leader, it was important to delegate authority, and the further authority could be pushed down, the better. Lee chose as his corps commanders General Longstreet, who already held corps command; General Richard Ewell, whom Lee called "an honest, brave soldier, who has always done his duty well"; and General Ambrose Powell Hill, "the best soldier of his grade with me."

Hill and Ewell were Virginians, West Pointers, and professional soldiers. They were also battle-tested commanders in the Army of Northern Virginia who had served under Stonewall Jackson. But the flip side of their combat experience was that Ewell had already lost a leg to amputation, following a combat wound, and A. P. Hill's health was beginning to falter under the stress of continuous campaigning. In addition, Ewell was high-strung and Hill had a tendency to impetuous action—qualities that Lee might have regarded as acceptable substitutes for Jackson's aggressive boldness, and even as a necessary counterpoint to Longstreet's stolidness.

General James Longstreet could be a bull in battle, but Lee had come to recognize that he also needed more direction and prodding than Jackson had. As a strategist, Lee was "audacity personified," while Longstreet was careful, cautious, and deliberate. Longstreet was also stubborn, which served him well when he was conducting a defensive battle, but it was a problem when his ideas conflicted with Lee's. While Lee could count on Jackson to execute the most daring operations, Longstreet was reluctant to take risks. At Gettysburg, this would prove fatal to Confederate hopes.

As the men marched across the Potomac and into Union territory, Lee again forbade "wanton injury to private property" and ordered that the soldiers pay civilians for what they needed. As always, the Confederate army was short of virtually everything. Horses and men were ragged. Gettysburg, the climactic battle of the war, would be fought because a Confederate brigade went to the town looking for shoes.

THE FIRST DAY

The battle was fought over three days, with the final troop totals equaling close to 95,000 Federals and 75,000 Confederates. As the initial skirmishes began, almost accidentally, Union General John Buford secured the high ground for the Federals. The Federal line eventually extended from the summits of Big Round Top and Little Round Top on the Union left, straight down Cemetery Ridge, curling in like the base of a J on the Federal right at Cemetery Hill and Culp's Hill.

On the first day of battle, as he rode up to investigate the action that had suddenly erupted, Lee inspected the ground. The Confederates were shoving the Federals from their advanced positions in front of Gettysburg and along Seminary Ridge. As the Federals took up their new line, which would often be called "the fishhook" because of its shape, Lee saw that an assault on the Union right, at the curve of the J, would allow the Confederates to sweep the line. He ordered General Ewell to attack that point "if practicable" without sparking a major battle. The "if practicable" was a common phrase in

Lee's orders, leaving discretion to the commander in the field; and in this case, Lee was eager to avoid a full-fledged engagement because so many Confederate troops were still on the march. Nevertheless, as the afternoon wore on, Lee's patience wore thin, as Ewell's front remained remarkably quiet.

Up to this point, Ewell had been an excellent combat soldier. But the wooden-legged veteran was no longer the same man. Always emotional, he was upset by the surprise action at Gettysburg. It had forced his recall from his own planned offensive at Harrisburg, Pennsylvania's capital, where Lee had sent him to threaten the rail lines. But "Old Baldy" couldn't translate one aggressive plan into another. Instead, he fell into pale irresolution. He had decided it wasn't practicable to take Cemetery Hill and Culp's Hill, though they had yet to be fully defended by the Federals. Ewell's men had already spent much of the day in combat—Ewell himself received a minié ball in his wooden leg—pushing the Federals back. He was reluctant to ask more of them. But had Ewell acted with a vigorous advance on these vital positions, he almost surely would have succeeded, and the entire Union line would have been in danger. Indeed, one of Ewell's generals had to be ordered four times to halt. As Confederate general John B. Gordon explained: "The whole portion of the Union army in my front was in inextricable confusion and in flight . . . my troops were upon the flank and sweeping down the lines. The firing upon my men had almost ceased. Large bodies of the Union troops were throwing down their arms and surrendering. . . . In less than half an hour my troops would have swept up and over those hills. . . . It is not surprising that . . . I should have refused at first to obey the order."

Daylight was fading, and Ewell and his subordinates told Lee that it was too late for an assault. Lee pressed them: "Can't you, with your corps, attack on daylight tomorrow?" Ewell, along with his tough generals Rodes and Early, thought not. Their men were tired, the hill increasingly fortified. They wanted to hold their line, and take up the defensive. Even Jubal A. Early, a hard fighter, wanted to shift the burden of attack to someone else. He thought the better plan would be for Longstreet to strike the opposite flank, which was yet to be fortified. If Longstreet could take Little Round Top, it would achieve the same result of allowing the Confederates to sweep Cemetery Ridge.

Lee was shocked. His second corps, his offensive thunderbolt, old Stonewall's command, had grown battle weary. He had no objection to Early's plan in principle—indeed, it was the plan he would execute—but he worried about Longstreet, his defensive counterpuncher, having to carry it out. As Lee said: "Well, if I attack from my right, Longstreet will have to make the attack. Longstreet is a very good fighter when he gets in position and gets everything ready, but he is so slow." Lee's assessment of Longstreet was correct; though attacking from his right made perfect sense, Lee always considered the human factor—and Longstreet was not the commander one would choose for such a maneuver.

Still, Lee was also disinclined to override Ewell, Rodes, and Early, who would have to make the assault on his left. They were generally aggressive commanders. If they did not think his assignment could be done . . . well, he found it hard to think that it couldn't, but he decided not to press the issue, at least not now. Longstreet would simply have to lift the burden of attack. The land and the disposition of the Union army favored his assault, and Longstreet was a reliable, professional soldier. There was no reason Longstreet should not succeed.

Meanwhile, Lee assumed that Ewell and his lieutenants would snap out of their malaise after a night's rest. He left them orders for the next day: to demonstrate on their front, while Lee launched an attack on the opposite end of the

Union line. If practicable, Ewell's men should turn the demonstration into a full-fledged attack.

Later that night Ewell rode to Lee's headquarters, abashed at his performance, and assured his commander that he would attack Culp's Hill in the morning. That was more like it, Lee thought. He reassured Ewell that his attack would still be in support of Longstreet's main assault on the Union left. Lee's plan was to "attack the enemy in the morning as soon as possible." If Ewell's men were up to it, Lee could attempt to turn the Union left *and* the Union right, crumpling the Union line.

Though battle had come accidentally, Lee was convinced that this was the showdown he had long expected and had tried to force. As Lee told General Hood: "The enemy is here, and if we do not whip him, he will whip us." It was on this field that the Army of Northern Virginia might crush the Army of the Potomac and effectively end the war.

THE SECOND DAY

Overall, Lee's troops had performed well on the first day. It was the Federals, after all, who had given ground. If Ewell's failure to seize the high ground on the Union right had been costly, Lee saw another opportunity on the Union left, where the Federals had yet to occupy Big Round Top and Little Round Top. If he could get Longstreet's men up there first, he could drive the Federals from their position, their flank would be turned, and the swelling tide of the Confederacy would rise even higher.

Longstreet, however, was to reveal his fatal weakness, one for which Lee found it difficult to compensate. Longstreet disliked Lee's plan, preferring, according to his later testimony, to maneuver the Confederate army into a defensive position that would force the Yankees to attack it. Though he was

Lee's subordinate officer, Longstreet expressed his disapproval of Lee's plan through his surly sluggardness in preparing his troops for the assault. Longstreet was always slow, but generally had the excuse that he would launch a well-prepared strike when truly needed. At Gettysburg, however, his laggardness betrayed an insubordinate hope: if he moved slowly enough, the whole plan of attack might be called off.

At 8:30 A.M., Lee rode up to Longstreet and told him flatly, "I think you had better move on." Thinking that was clear enough instruction, he rode back to direct Ewell, whose nerves were jangling again. By 10 A.M., Lee was back at the center of the Confederate line. To his dismay, Longstreet's guns weren't firing, and his men weren't moving. Lee rode to Longstreet's position. It was now 11 A.M. Longstreet had done nothing because with his usual caution he had decided to wait until he could be joined by General Pickett, and his corps be brought closer to full strength. "The general," Longstreet explained to one of his officers, "wishes me to attack; I do not wish to do so without Pickett. I never like to go into battle with one boot off." Pickett, however, would not be able to reach the field until the end of the day.

Lee ordered Longstreet forward. The correspondent for the *Times* of London, Francis Lawley, wrote, "Lee struck me as more anxious and ruffled than I had ever seen him before, though it required close observation to detect it."

Still Longstreet failed to move. Another brigade under General Evander Law was due in half an hour. He told Lee he wanted those extra men. Lee reluctantly agreed, though the delay inevitably lengthened until one o'clock. When Longstreet's men finally began their advance, Lee again rode to the center of the line. Once engaged, Lee assumed that the bullish Longstreet would press the enemy. But he was wrong. Longstreet was still sulking, and moving slow. It was not until four o'clock that his men were in position to launch their attack.

By now circumstances had changed. Little Round Top was occupied. But General Hood, leading Lee's beloved Texans, knew what to do to compensate. He dispatched scouts to see if it was still possible to swing around the Union left as originally planned. The answer was yes, if the Confederates moved their attack to Big Round Top. Hood reported his intelligence to Longstreet. But Longstreet played the political general. If he was going to execute an order with which he disagreed, after all attempts to foil it by delay had sputtered, he would execute it to the letter so that if it failed no opprobrium would fall on him. Longstreet's generals asked him to reconsider, reminding him that Lee's orders were for an attack in the morning. The situation had changed, but the spirit, if not the letter, of the order could be fulfilled with an easily executable maneuver. Longstreet stubbornly refused. He sent his men charging, in echelon, uphill, into spewing Union fire. The assault, though bravely attempted, was ill-coordinated, with reserve units that could have made a difference left doing nothing.

As the day closed, Lee remained optimistic despite the almost blackly comical situation confronting him. On his left was a fidgety, one-legged general, "Old Baldy" Ewell, once a fighter, now wracked by indecisiveness. At his center was fierce A. P. Hill with his famous red battle shirt. But Hill, whose health was beginning its long slide, was recovering from another bout of illness. On Lee's right was his formerly dependable "old war horse" General Longstreet. But Longstreet, apparently giving full vent to a corrupting egotism now that he was removed from Stonewall Jackson's shadow, was behaving like a sulking Achilles—his actions verging on, if not exactly defining, insubordination.

Then there was Lee's beloved cavalry commander, Jeb Stuart, waving his plumed hat in another ride around the Yankee army, returning with wagons full of captured supplies, but too late to be the desperately needed eyes and ears of Lee's army. And Lee himself was unwell, afflicted with "camp stomach" and the undiagnosed heart disease that made him feel "more and more incapable of physical exertion" and that would eventually take his life.

Despite all this, Lee remained optimistic, because although his attacks had failed, he knew the Federals felt hard-pressed on both ends of their line. And Lee had now spotted their vulnerable point—dead center, the weakest point in the Union fishhook. If he could punch through it, he could scatter the then-divided Union forces. His plan was for Ewell to launch a diversionary attack on the Union right, while Longstreet brought his men to an attack on the Union center. It was to prove the most controversial battle plan of the war, and gave birth to America's own Charge of the Light Brigade, Pickett's Charge.

THE THIRD DAY

After Lee's death, Longstreet claimed that he had had an alternative plan, which he had presented to his commanding general. Under Longstreet's plan, the Confederate army would have declined engagement at Gettysburg and positioned itself between Meade's army and its line of retreat to Washington, allowing the Confederates to take up defensive positions that could easily repel a Union attack. In its own way, it was a daring plan, if perhaps unrealistic, given the dangers of maneuvering and subsisting in enemy territory. One obvious flaw to the plan was that it was not necessarily Meade who would be cut off from retreat, but the Confederates; Meade could have simply isolated Lee's army, besieged it with his superior numbers, and waited for it to starve. Moreover, Meade was ready (if worried, as he noted later) should the Confederate army attempt the difficult maneuver, and could have hit the Confederates in transit as they attempted to take up their positions. Though Longstreet's plan has became popularly accepted as the better one by readers influenced by critics of Lee and by Michael Shaara's brilliant novel *The Killer Angels* and its faithful and spectacular screen adaptation *Gettysburg*, it was not incontestably so. In fact, there is every reason to believe that Lee's plan was the right one.

Not only had he accurately diagnosed where the Union line was weak, Lee had succeeded with a similar attack a year earlier at Gaines' Mill southwest of Richmond. At Gaines' Mill, Lee stretched the Union line with assaults by Longstreet at one end and D. H. Hill on the other. Lee then ordered General Hood to attack the center and break the Union line.

"This must be done," Lee said. "Can you do it?"

"I can try," Hood replied.

The frontal attack at Gaines' Mill was a tremendous risk. The charge would be against entrenched Federal positions, in the teeth of artillery fire, and over the bodies of the wounded and dying of A. P. Hill's six brigades, whose own impetuous charges had fallen short. If Lee failed, his army would be gravely weakened and the Union forces could have resumed their advance on Richmond. But at Gaines' Mill, in the words of his biographer Clifford Dowdey, "Lee demonstrated . . . his willingness to risk a decisive defeat in committing himself to win." It was a style of operation that would typify Lee's aggressiveness as a commander.

At Lee's order, Hood threw his men into the battle, over the bloody ground, where the wounded from A. P. Hill's brigades grabbed frantically at the Texans' pant legs, trying to stop what they could only consider a suicidal assault. But the

Texans, reinforced by Georgians under the command of Evander Law, surged forward, screaming the Rebel Yell, ignoring the shells bursting around them, their own firearms silent, not wanting to break stride until they pierced the Union line. And pierce it they did, breaking the first line, then the second line. The Union soldiers turned and ran. Only darkness saved the Federals, who scampered across the Chickahominy River.

Gaines' Mill resulted in Lee's first major victory, the beginning of a series of victories that drove McClellan away from Richmond in the Seven Days campaign. Now he was to try the same battle-tested strategy again.

In the morning, Ewell's men and A. P. Hill's men were ready. But there was no word from Longstreet. Lee rode to "Old Pete" and found his subordinate again ready to argue with him. Longstreet had decided that he wanted to renew his flanking attack; or, if one goes by his postwar writings, actually shift Lee's entire army to the Union's left flank to "maneuver him into attacking us."

Lee could have cashiered Longstreet on the spot. The "old Dutchman" had ignored Lee's orders, ignored the disposition of the other two corps of the army, and was preparing to launch his own independent assault. But Lee was patient. He was short of good officers, and Longstreet had been one of his best. In his battle report, Lee merely noted that "General Longstreet's dispositions were not completed as early as expected."

Lee listened to Longstreet's proposal of an alternative flanking movement, rejected it, and ordered him to take up his position as ordered. Longstreet reluctantly complied, but not before making one final verbal sally to stop his commander's plan. "General, I have been a soldier all my life. I have been with soldiers engaged in fights by couples, by squads, companies, regiments, divisions, and armies, and should know as well as anyone what soldiers can do. It is my opinion that no 15,000 men ever arrayed for battle can take that position."

Lee, as always, heard his subordinate out. But he remained convinced that Longstreet's protests were ill-advised. Lee rode along the line, pointing out the potential strength of the Confederate assault. The infantry would advance under cover of the largest artillery bombardment ever attempted by the Confederate army. Eight of Longstreet's thirteen brigades would be committed to the attack, leaving a plentiful reserve to be committed later as needed, and to receive a Federal counterattack, should Longstreet fail.

Among those committed to the attack would be the three fresh brigades, numbering 4,600 men, under the command of General George Pickett. Every man in the division was a Virginian. Pickett was a dandy—the Confederate version of General Custer—with perfumed, ringleted hair, an abysmal academic record at West Point, and an eagerness for action. His brigade commanders were:

+ James L. Kemper, a lawyer and former member of the Virginia House of Delegates whose grandfather had served on General George Washington's staff
+ Richard B. Garnett, another dashing West Point graduate from a distinguished Virginia family, who would ride in Pickett's charge, however dangerous a target that made him, because of a bad knee and a worse fever that kept him from marching
+ Lewis A. Armistead, the most famous of the brigadiers (after the events of this day), one of whose best friends, General W. S. Hancock, was facing him on the Union line

The soldiers were aware that everything that had gone before was climaxing here. It was an epic moment, and a desperate one; the fate of the Confederate States of America, its very existence, might be determined here. It was impossible to think that men who had fought so well in the campaigns thus far, against such tremendous odds, would not triumph when the stakes were so high.

The troops took up their positions under sheltering shade trees and waited, shielded from the Federals' sight by a short rise in the ground in front of them. As Lee rode along the line, he saw his fresh Virginians, but he also saw the other troops that would be committed to the attack. Some of them had endured hard fighting in the last two days, and were bandaged or limping. Indeed, so many had been mauled or killed that of the 15,000 men Lee expected to make the charge, the true number was no more than 12,000 effectives. Lee himself said, "Many of these poor boys should go to the rear; they are not able for duty." He quietly noted the absence of many familiar faces, officers and friends, now dead. He wished the men well and told them, "The attack must succeed."

Shortly after one o'clock in the afternoon, the Confederate artillery barrage began. The artillery was under the command of a talented 28-year-old Georgian, Colonel Edward Porter Alexander, on whom General Longstreet, quite unfairly, attempted to shove responsibility for the coming action.

Longstreet had dispatched him a note with these instructions: "If the artillery fire does not have the effect to drive off the enemy or greatly demoralize him, so as to make our effort pretty certain, I would prefer that you should not advise Pickett to make the charge. I shall rely a great deal upon your judgment to determine the matter and shall expect you to let General Pickett know when the moment offers."

It was not Colonel Alexander's responsibility to advise Pickett, it was Longstreet's. But Old Pete appeared yet again to be attempting to subvert Lee's plans and to recruit doubters fearful of taking responsibility for the charge.

Alexander's response to Longstreet was a simple statement of fact and a reminder that his job was to execute plans, not draw them up and decide which ones to implement: "General, I will only be able to judge of the effect of our fire on the enemy by his return fire, for his infantry is but little exposed to view and the smoke will obscure the whole field. If, as I infer from your note, there is any alternative to this attack, it should be carefully considered before opening our fire, for it will take all the artillery ammunition we have left to test this one thoroughly, and if the result is unfavorable, we will have none left for another effort."

Longstreet stubbornly kept the pressure on the young man, replying, "The intention is to advance the infantry if the artillery has the desired effect of driving the enemy's [artillery] off, or having other effect such as to warrant us in making the attack. When that moment arrives advise General P., and of course advance such artillery as you can use in aiding the attack."

The colonel submitted. "When our fire is best, I will advise General Pickett to advance."

Longstreet ordered the cannonade to begin, and a rain of shrieking, exploding lead burst over the Union lines. It made a splendid racket, but as the smoke thickened, the Confederate gunners were firing blindly and largely overshooting their mark. The havoc they wreaked was largely on the rear of the Union army, not the men at the front.

Less than a half hour into the bombardment, Colonel Alexander tried to urge Pickett forward. "If you are coming at all," his note read, "you must come at once, or I cannot give you proper support." Ten minutes later, seeing no movement on the Confederate line, he sent another dispatch. "For God's sake come quick. . . . Come quick or I can't support you." While Alexander knew full well the difficulties the

Confederates faced in their charge at the Union center, he also saw a glimmer of opportunity, as the Federals were attempting to maneuver their own artillery to safety. If Pickett moved now, he might move under a brief artillery advantage.

But Pickett did not move because he had no orders from Longstreet. Alexander's bombardment continued until 2:45 P.M., when he ordered a cease fire. By three o'clock the Confederate troops were finally marching forward. They had never received an order from Longstreet to move out; Old Pete limited himself to a sober nod of the head when Pickett requested permission to advance.

In fact, Longstreet's dilatory tactics had again bollixed up the execution of Lee's plan. Colonel Alexander had now expended too much ammunition. There was not enough to adequately support the Confederate advance. As had happened the day before, Longstreet's delays, his hope against hope that the plans he disagreed with would be cancelled, resulted only in the plans being executed in the worst possible way.

Lee learned a hard lesson at Gettysburg. Jackson, who would have executed Lee's plans with all the vigor he desired, was irreplaceable. The lesson was, again, that people count. In any organization personnel *is* policy, and it is wrong to trust to subordinates who do not fully share a leader's vision. The result will nearly always be half-hearted, faulty execution and even subversion—however well-intentioned—of one's plans.

The Confederates now had the challenge of crossing a mile of open ground with minimal artillery support to suppress Federal fire. They did not flinch. Officers to the front, General Armistead shoved his black hat over the tip of his sword and waved his men forward.

Now—now that it was too late—Longstreet joined Colonel Alexander to find out why the Confederate guns were silent. Alexander informed him. He was saving what little ammunition he had left so that he could offer at least some support for the Confederate advance. Longstreet was shocked. Pickett's men should have been ordered forward an hour and a half earlier. Now they were marching into a maw of doom. "Go and stop Pickett right where he is, and replenish your ammunition!" Longstreet commanded.

But that was impossible. "We can't do that, sir. The train has but little. It would take an hour to distribute it, and meanwhile the enemy would improve the time."

Longstreet shook his head sorrowfully. He mumbled a mournful confession, "I do not want to make this charge. I do not see how it can succeed. I would not make it now but that General Lee has ordered it and expects it."

It might have been better if Longstreet had not allowed his melancholy to overcome him, encouraging him to drag his feet—if he'd remembered the old saw that he who hesitates is lost. *That* was the apropos tag, which Lee and Jackson understood, but which Longstreet was constitutionally unable to see and avoid.

The Confederates marched forward as if on parade, even stopping at one point to adjust and straighten their lines, oblivious to the holes being torn in their ranks by the Union fire. For the Union troops, the Confederates were marching through a shooting gallery, but they could not believe the grandeur of the spectacle as the troops moved relentlessly forward, their flags held high. A British observer, Lt. Colonel Arthur Fremantle of Her Majesty's Coldstream Guards, made the mistake of expressing his excitement and admiration to Longstreet. "I wouldn't have missed this for anything," Fremantle said.

Longstreet, who had a streak of gallows humor in him, laughed and replied, "The devil you wouldn't! I would like to have missed this very much."

The attack, Longstreet told Fremantle, had already failed: "The charge is over." Indeed, the unthinkable had occurred. Four Confederate regiments, and Virginia ones at that, broke and ran under heavy shell fire. They were already mauled units from Henry Heth's division, at half-strength since Chancellorsville, under temporary officers (Heth himself had been wounded on the first day of Gettysburg), and they were exhausted. Yet the shock for every Confederate officer, save Longstreet, was profound.

But the shock was also temporary. The remainder of the Confederate line, including the rest of Heth's division (now under the command of the remarkable 35-year-old North Carolinian General James J. Pettigrew, classical scholar, athlete, linguist, lawyer, and now soldier), marched on, the officers and men maintaining their disciplined coolness under fire. As the historian Shelby Foote has written, "Southern courtesy had never been more severely tried, yet such protest as was heard was mild in tone. It was here that the classic Confederate line was spoken: 'Move on, cousins. You are drawing the fire our way.'"

Of Pickett's Virginians, Brigadier Garnett was shot off his horse, dead. Brigadier Kemper, calling for Armistead's men to support his brigade—he thought he just might carry his men through the Union line—collapsed, shot in the groin.

The Confederates were close enough now to break into a jog. The Rebel Yell finally rose from the brave frontline North Carolinians, who were immediately blasted by Union canister, and struck by fire on two sides.

But for all the smoke, artillery fire, minié balls, and disaster that enveloped the Confederates, the Union front *was* suddenly pierced. Chasing after a line of retreating Federals was General Armistead, still waving his black hat on his sword, shouting, "Come on, boys! Give them the cold steel! Follow me!" They surged forward into hand-to-hand combat, Armistead and his men running straight into two Federal regiments rushing to close the line. Armistead, arm outstretched to a silent Federal cannon, went down, mortally wounded, falling at a point on the battlefield now called "the high tide of the Confederacy." Many of his men either fell with him or were captured. On another part of the front, the University Greys, made up entirely of students from Ole Miss, managed to plant their colors no more than a yard from the Union line, before the devastating Union fire killed every last one of them.

Now it really was over. The Confederate lines wavered and buckled. The few men that breached the stone wall that marked the Federal line were quickly taken prisoner. Even the most aggressive officers knew they could no longer overwhelm the Federal position. As one rebel commander said, "The best thing the men can do is get out of this. Let them go."

As the shattered Confederate units drifted back, Lee rode forward to meet them. "All this will come right in the end," he assured them. "All good men must rally. . . . General Pickett . . . your men have done all that men could do; the fault is entirely my own. . . . All this has been my fault—it is I that have lost this fight and you must help me out of it the best way you can."

To Lt. Colonel Fremantle, Lee said, "This has been a sad day for us, Colonel, a sad day. But we can't always expect to win victories." Fremantle noted that as the Confederates fell into their defensive positions around Lee, he "saw many badly wounded men take off their hats and cheer him."

There were no recriminations from Lee against Longstreet or Ewell or any of the others. All blame he took upon his own shoulders. Lee knew that however much discretion he left to his officers in the field, ultimately the responsibility was his. It was no good assigning blame anyway—a waste of time, a distraction from what really mattered. The danger confronting the Army of Northern Virginia was far from past. Lee had to be ready for a Federal counterattack.

But the attack did not come. General Meade was overjoyed that he had turned back the charge, and he had no intention of going on the offensive. He could barely believe his luck, that he had apparently succeeded where every other general before him—McClellan, "the young Napoleon"; Pope, who boasted his headquarters would be in his saddle, and who carried that saddle back as fast as he could to the North; Burnside, commander of the "Mud March"; and "Fighting Joe" Hooker, who fought his way in frantic retreat from an army less than half his size—had failed.

On the Confederate side of the line, meanwhile, Longstreet finally roused his better self. Like Lee, he rode among his men, encouraging them, and readying them for the expected counterattack. His gloomy spirits were shaken off. He was ready to fight the sort of battle he preferred, a defensive one.

But it was too late for any fighting now. Both sides were licking deep wounds. The Union army had suffered 23,000 casualties. For the Confederates, the statistics were even grimmer. Twenty-eight thousand men were lost, more than a third of Lee's army. Among them, a high proportion of senior officers, men whose talents and experience could not be replaced any time soon. As one British observer noted of Lee's army, "Your troops do wonders, but every time at a cost you cannot afford."

Lee undoubtedly shared this opinion, for it was the very purpose of his strategy at Gettysburg to fight the climactic battle that would finish off the Army of the Potomac and bring peace. Now that plan itself was finished; it lay in ashes on the bloodiest battlefield of the war.

With darkness closing in, Lee retired to his tent and drew up his plans for retreat. Reflecting on the disillusioning experience of the last few days, his orders were detailed and firm, leaving his officers no room for discretion. Delegation had served him well in the past, but he was not sure he could trust to it in the future.

At 1:00 A.M., he rode out to join cavalry general John D. Imboden, who would be supervising the retreating wagon trains.

The strain of the day began to show, and Lee's customary reserve faded as the two men talked. At one point Lee said: "I never saw troops behave more magnificently than Pickett's division of Virginians did today in that grand charge upon the enemy. And if they had been supported as they were to have been—but for some reason not yet fully explained to me, were not—we would have held the position and the day would have been ours. Too bad. Too bad! Oh, too bad!"

With that mild exclamation, Lee marked the grave where he buried his dreams of ending the war quickly. He turned in his saddle and said tiredly, "We must now return to Virginia." He knew the war was far from over.

LEE'S LESSONS

+ A leader, in delegating authority, should never trust to the discretion of a subordinate who does not share his vision.

+ A leader needs to remember that even the best soldiers can be pushed too far and their limits strained. As Lee told Longstreet the day after the battle of Gettysburg, "It's all my fault. I thought my men were invincible."

• A leader takes full responsibility for the failures on his watch, and never tries to shift blame to his subordinates. A leader's job is not to assign blame but to make the best of every circumstance and to meet every new challenge to his objective.

CHAPTER EIGHT

LEE VERSUS GRANT

AFTER SHARPSBURG, Lee retained his optimism that he could defeat the Union army at will. After Gettysburg, the Confederate task became one of grim survival. Lee no longer had the men, the horses, or the provisions to attempt another invasion of the North. He was now compelled to fight on the defensive. His task: to repel the invader at every turn. Remarkably, he did.

The army, of course, was vulnerable after the blood-letting at Gettysburg. But Meade's pursuit of Lee's men was hampered by heavy rain. Moreover, it was wary and half-hearted. In the words of one Confederate staff officer, the Federals "pursued us as a mule goes on the chase after a grizzly bear—as if catching up with us was the last thing he wanted."

But if Meade retained a respectful caution toward the Army of Northern Virginia, Lee was facing a series of calamities. His own army, of course, had taken horrible losses. But he soon learned that in the west, concurrent with the battle of Gettysburg, Union General Ulysses S. Grant had broken the Confederates at Vicksburg, Mississippi, after a long siege that had been so severe it had compelled the people to live in caves dug into the hills. The Union now owned the Mississippi

River, and was even pushing the Confederates out of Tennessee.

On a personal note, Lee's son Rooney was now a prisoner of war, the latest in an awful sequence of events for the Lee family. Since the war began Lee had suffered the death of one of his young children and two of his grandchildren. He would soon lose a daughter-in-law. His wife was crippled. Virtually all his material possessions had been either confiscated or destroyed. His one last possession, his army, was in retreat; its cause in peril. And as if defending against a Union attack were not enough to worry about, President Davis alerted Lee to the fact that he was also under fire from the press for his failure to secure victory at Gettysburg.

Lee would note, with remarkable good humor in the bleak days toward the end of the war, "We made a great mistake in the beginning of our struggle, and I fear, in spite of all we can do, it will prove to be a fatal mistake. We appointed all our worst generals to command our armies, and all our best generals to edit the newspapers."

Lee gave Davis his frank assessment of the battle:

No blame can be attached to the army for its failure to accomplish what was projected by me, nor should it be censured for the unreasonable expectations of the public. I am alone to blame, in perhaps expecting too much of its prowess and valour. . . . I thought at the time that . . . [victory] was practicable. I still think if all things could have worked together it would have been accomplished.

But with the knowledge I had then, and in the circumstances I was then placed, I do not know what better course I could have pursued.

Roughly a week later, Lee offered to resign.

Davis responded immediately, writing Lee: "To ask me to substitute you by some one in my judgement more fit to command, or who would possess more of the confidence of the army, or of the reflecting men of the country, is to demand an impossibility."

Lee remained in his position. As for himself, he had no doubts about the course he took at Gettysburg. He even felt that Meade had taken the worst of the fighting. He told one interlocutor, "We did whip them at Gettysburg, and it will be seen for the next six months that that army will be as quiet as a sucking dove"—a prediction that proved correct.

But Lee also recognized that the last day of Gettysburg was his greatest gamble; his throw of the dice to end the war. In that, it had failed. It was only fitting, therefore, to offer to make way for someone else with other plans, if President Davis saw fit. But President Davis, astutely, did not. He kept his weary commander on the job, advising him, "Take all possible care of yourself."

And to remind his countrymen of what was appropriate behavior in this time of trial, President Davis proclaimed a day of "fasting, humiliation, and prayer." It was a time, Davis implied, not for blame, recrimination, and editorial carping, but for soul-searching and for seeking God's blessing for the Confederate cause.

Though buttressed by Davis's support, Lee's health was increasingly unsteady. Until the war, he had rarely been sick. Now his body was tired, worn out, afflicting him with pain and discomfort. Nevertheless, his spirit remained undaunted. Less than two months after Gettysburg, less than a month after he had offered to resign, Lee was writing Longstreet "to use every exertion to bring General Meade out and use our efforts to crush his army while it is in its present condition."

But because of setbacks in the west, the Army of Northern Virginia was further depleted of men. Longstreet and the bulk of his corps were sent to fight for Tennessee. The remainder of his corps went to the defense of Charleston, South Carolina.

Still, Lee, with only 47,000 men, remained a tiger, eager to strike at the 77,000 Federals Meade had marched into Northern Virginia.

But Meade would not be drawn. When Lee tried to maneuver Meade into battle, Meade refused to meet him. At first, Lee kept his men on the march, pursuing Meade toward Washington. When that proved impractical, Lee's men dug in near the Rapidan River, hoping to lure Meade into an attack. Meade came close, but wouldn't take the bait.

So Lee varied his strategy, keeping his fortified line, hoping to hold Meade in front of him, but sending a strike force round to hit Meade's flank. Meade, however, withdrew, leaving the aggressive Lee frustrated. "I am too old to command this army," he said, "we should never have permitted those people to get away"—a fittingly combative assessment from a commander seeking to force into battle an army that outnumbered him by at least 30,000 men. Strikingly, Meade, with all his advantages in numbers and supplies, seemed to count his success in *avoiding* Lee—compelling testimony to the fact that the Confederate general's reputation for smashing Union troops and wrecking their generals' careers had suffered no setback at Gettysburg.

The Union and Confederate armies eventually settled into winter quarters, and Lee devoted himself to patching up his tattered men. "I have had to disperse the cavalry as much as possible to obtain forage for their horses," he wrote his wife. "Provisions for the men too are very scarce, and what with light diet and light clothing I fear they suffer. But still they are cheerful and uncomplaining." In that, the army reflected its commander. For Lee himself, with all his frustrations and personal sufferings, for all his gathering pessimism about the final outcome of the war, remained more than stoic, he was buoyant; his personal correspondence brightened by humorous sallies and lighthearted teasing.

Lee had developed his own character to focus on making the best of things; it was his duty as a leader to follow that path, and Lee believed that in executing his duty he was fulfilling his purpose as a man under God. He took, as a matter of course, that "satisfaction that proceeds from the consciousness of duty faithfully performed." It was the one reward that Lee expected all leaders to enjoy.

Lee's front remained largely quiescent until late spring. His army rebuilt itself, with the return of Longstreet's corps, to approximately 62,000 men. But the Federals had increased their own numbers even more rapidly. In March, President Lincoln had called for 700,000 new troops—more than ten times Lee's current strength. Lee already faced a Union army of almost twice his size, roughly 119,000 men; and one of them was General Ulysses S. Grant, the new general-in-chief of all Union armies.

But however large their numbers, whoever was now their ultimate field commander, Lee planned to harass *them*, rather than waiting for them to attack him. "If we could take the initiative and fall upon them unexpectedly," Lee wrote Davis, "we might derange their plans and embarrass them the whole summer."

This was the Lee of old, but the tenor of the war was changing. In Grant, Lee would find an opponent willing to suffer virtually limitless effusions of blood to wear the Confederate commander down in a war of hard-slogging attrition. Grant knew that time was on his side. Even in cavalry, where the Confederates had held an unparalleled edge with their splendid horsemen, the Union was now in the ascendant, with an unending supply of fresh, strong horses to challenge Confederate mounts that were going hungry, and that were hard to replace if killed.

And there were other changes. Lee had always opposed the Union's tactics of total war, but these too were increasing, under the lash of frustration and strife. The South would soon be suffering under General William Tecumseh Sherman's fiery "March to the Sea" and Union General Phil Sheridan's farm-burning crusade in the Shenandoah Valley. March 1864 opened with the ominous news that a band of Yankee raiders had been captured near Richmond. On the body of their dead commander were papers indicating their intention to kill the most prominent Confederate civilian of all, President Jefferson Davis.

Lee had every reason to redouble his determination to fight "those people," who were waging war not only against his army but also against the laws of civilization, against civilians. Every elderly man, every woman, and every child in the Confederacy was at risk. Lee had to worry not only about attrition to his army, but about the eroding constraints on what was regarded as acceptable violence as the war dragged on.

Grant's plan for the opening of the 1864 campaign was to use his large army to, at a minimum, fence Lee in—if he couldn't defeat him or get around him to attack Richmond—while the Union maintained its inexorable advance in every other theater of the war, all lines eventually converging on the Confederate capital. Grant wanted to ensure that Lee would not again invade Union territory—which was now unlikely in any event—and make it impossible for him to assist Confederate detachments in the Shenandoah Valley or in southside Virginia, where other Federal armies could squeeze the Confederates out through sheer force of numbers.

THE WILDERNESS

Grant's army advanced on Lee's positions, marching through a heavily wooded area west of Fredericksburg known as the

Wilderness. Lee was only too happy to meet him there. For in the Wilderness, Lee surmised, the dense forest would negate much of Grant's numerical superiority. In fact, he might even trap the Federal army.

Lee's first challenge was that his army was at only two-thirds strength. Longstreet's corps was a day's march away. Nevertheless, Ewell's and A. P. Hill's corps rushed to engage the Federals and pin them down in the Wilderness in the expectation that Longstreet would soon come up. On the first day of fighting, Hill—outnumbered nearly three to one—caught and held the Federals on his front. As night fell, the Confederates, tired by hard marching and even harder fighting, drifted, exhausted, to sleep. A. P. Hill had fought well, but again was sick.

Lee's offensive mind took little notice of the weakness of his lines, stretched thin against a massive Union force. He hoped to take Longstreet's fresh troops and reenact the Confederate victory at Chancellorsville, launching a flank attack on the Federal Goliath trapped in the Wilderness.

But Longstreet was late.

At 5:00 A.M., a massive Federal assault tore into the ragged Confederate lines. Grant had seen his opportunity to rip Lee's tired army to pieces.

Lee quickly mounted his horse and rode to the front to rally his men. He knew that at this moment, if the Federals burst through, the Army of Northern Virginia could be finished. Butternut uniforms were streaming past him, the men recoiling from the shock of the Union assault.

"My God, General McGowan," Lee shouted, "is this splendid brigade of yours running like a flock of geese?"

Lee was answered not by McGowan, but by Longstreet's lead troops running onto the field.

Lee waved them forward. "Who are you, my boys?"

"Texas boys!"

"Hurrah for Texas!" Lee took his hat and thrust it in the air. "Hurrah for Texas!"

Lee himself led the Texans to their positions, riding his horse directly behind them as they advanced.

"Go back, General Lee! Lee to the rear!"

But Lee did not go back. There was a blaze in his eye. All the continuing pressures of this war had now compounded into Lee's soul a sense that this was his war, his personal defense needed to be made for old Virginia. He would ride to the front, and with his gauntleted hand strike his own personal blow against the invader.

"General Lee, you must get back."

One of his aides, Colonel Venable, took Traveller's bridle. Lee would not go of his own accord or at the request of the men. Lee and Traveller had to be forcibly evicted.

Longstreet may have been late, but he made up for it by pressing the battle aggressively, not merely repelling the Union charge, but crumpling the Federals' left flank. So effective was the Confederate countercharge that it appeared the momentum would be completely turned—that the moment of absolute Confederate danger might become an amazing Confederate triumph, routing the Union forces.

But it was not the flanking movement of Chancellorsville that was reenacted, it was the tragedy of Jackson, as General Longstreet was felled, riding ahead of his lines, badly wounded by friendly fire. With Longstreet down, Lee again rode to the front to direct the Confederate attack, but he found the forward surge of the Confederate line had already stalled. The moment of redirecting it had passed—yet not before teaching Grant the likely cost of trying to cage Lee's Confederate tigers.

With the smallest army Lee had fielded, he inflicted more casualties then he had on Burnside at Fredericksburg or on

Hooker at Chancellorsville. The Wilderness, in fact, was a stunning tactical victory, though Lee was again frustrated that he was prevented from reaping its full potential.

In the battle of the Wilderness, Grant lost nearly two men for every one of Lee's (Union casualties were 18,000 to not quite 11,000 for the Confederates). But it was a ratio that Grant knew he could afford and still, over time, emerge the victor.

Lee understood Grant's mind as well as he had that of the other Union generals he had faced. McClellan in these circumstances would have pulled his army out, refitted his men, and entrenched them, calling for more reinforcements. Pope and Hooker would have fled from the nightmarish brambles of the Wilderness and, on their way to Washington, clamored for more troops. Burnside would have pulled back and marched his men one way and the other outside the forest, stalling for time to see what orders might come from President Lincoln. Meade, who was actually here under Grant's command, might have held his ground and waited, if the choice had been his.

Lee knew that Grant would choose none of these options. Grant would not withdraw, he would attempt a relentless series of hooks to the body of Lee's army. He would shift his men to the left and attack, shift to the left and attack, forcing Lee to keep moving with him to block the Army of the Potomac from advancing against Richmond.

Lee summarized the situation for President Davis:

[Grant's] position is strongly entrenched, and we cannot attack it with any prospect of success without great loss of men which I wish to avoid if possible. The enemy's artillery is superior in weight of metal and range to our own, and my object has been to engage him when in motion and under circumstances that will not cause us to suffer from this disadvantage.

I think by this means he has suffered considerably in the several past combats. . . . I shall continue to strike him wherever opportunity presents itself. . . . Neither the strength of our army nor the condition of our animals will admit of any extensive movement with a view to drawing the enemy from his position. I think he is now waiting for reenforcements. . . . The importance of this campaign to the administration of Mr. Lincoln and to General Grant leaves no doubt that every effort and every sacrifice will be made to secure its success.

Lee would not be able to take the strategic initiative and wreck Grant's plans. He simply had too few men and too little room to maneuver. But Lee compensated for his every weakness in artillery, manpower, and fodder by seizing every conceivable advantage offered to him. An old Latin tag captures much of Lee's military vision: *carpe diem,* seize the day, seize opportunities when they appear. Or to sound again Lee's recurrent theme: don't dwell on weaknesses, make the most of whatever advantages you have. In Lee's case, what he could do—and what he did do—was to successfully parry every blow attempted by Grant, and bloody the Union general's nose in the bargain.

LEE TO THE FRONT

Lee's method of leadership also underwent a change. With Jackson dead, Longstreet out of action, A. P. Hill in continued bad health, and Ewell testing Lee's patience with his growing indecisiveness (which had afflicted Lee's plans in the Wilderness as it had at Gettysburg), Lee assumed more and more of a personal command of his shrinking army. There are times when a leader must personally assume detailed command. For

Lee, that time was now. For his men, it would be a time of supreme inspiration.

Lee's increasingly personal field command did not strike anyone who served with him as a variant of the self-assertion or egotism he despised. It was simply necessary after the attrition of his officer corps, and because Lee himself was a sterling field officer. In Mexico, he had shown an eye for ground that made difficult offensive maneuvers not only possible but successful. Now again he was riding the lines, confessing, "I have to do my own reconnaissance. I am so stupid that I cannot rely on others."

Lee, as we have seen, had a profound understanding of the necessity of delegation. But every leader must also have a firm grasp of the essentials of his business and of the changing environment in which he operates. The essentials of Lee's business over which he had immediate control were, of course, his men, whom he inspected at every opportunity. The changing environment was the land on which they fought. Every successful general from the Duke of Wellington to Rommel has felt the same: do your own reconnaissance. In business terms, know the hard facts of the marketplace, know the terrain occupied by you and your opponent—know it personally.

Similarly, all leaders will find they have some subordinates whose own eyes for terrain and the management of men are unsatisfactory. Another test of leadership is how to deal with these subordinates.

When it was necessary for Lee to replace officers who had lost his confidence, he was careful do so in ways that did not shame the officer in front of his men or utterly shatter the officer's self-esteem. Indeed, he was so diplomatic that, as Douglas Southall Freeman attests, General Jubal A. Early's proudest memory of the war was of the letter he received from Lee removing him from command. Lee's letter to Early read:

General,—My telegram will have informed you that I deem a change of commanders in your Department necessary; but it is due to your zealous and patriotic services that I should explain the reasons that prompted my action. The situation of affairs is such that we can neglect no means calculated to develop the resources we possess to the greatest extent, and make them as efficient as possible. To this end, it is essential that we should have the cheerful and hearty support of the people, and the full confidence of the soldiers, without which our efforts would be embarrassed and our means of resistance weakened. I have reluctantly arrived at the conclusion that you cannot command the united and willing cooperation which is so essential to success. Your reverses in the Valley, of which the public and the army judge chiefly by the results, have, I fear, impaired your influence both with the people and the soldiers, and would greatly add to the difficulties which will, under any circumstances, attend our military operations in S.W. Virginia. While my own confidence in your ability, zeal, and devotion to the cause is unimpaired, I have nevertheless felt that I could not oppose what seems to be the current of opinion, without injustice to your reputation and injury to the service. I therefore felt constrained to endeavor to find a commander who would be more likely to develop the strength and resources of the country, and inspire the soldiers with confidence; and to accomplish this purpose, I thought it proper to yield my own opinion, and to defer to that of those to whom alone we can look for support.

I am sure that you will understand and appreciate my motives, and no one will be more ready than yourself to acquiesce in any measures which the interests of the country may seem to require, regardless of all personal considerations.

Thanking you for the fidelity and energy with which you have always supported my efforts, and for the courage and devotion you have ever manifested in the service of the country,

> I am, very respectfully, and truly,
> Your obedient servant,
>
> R. E. Lee,
> General

Lee always preferred to transfer unsatisfactory officers to jobs where they could do no harm, rather than sack them or court-martial them. Lee suffered inevitable moments of frustration when he felt his orders were not being properly executed or when younger officers had failed to show enough fire—or the reverse, when hot-blooded officers allowed themselves to be lured into unwise attacks. But he was not vindictive against failure, if an officer had tried his best. He retained a realistic assessment of what could be expected from his officers and of the limited alternatives available to him. When General A. P. Hill wanted to court-martial one of his subordinate generals, Lee admonished him: "Now, General Hill, I would not do that. General Wright isn't a professional soldier; he is a lawyer. He has come out here, fighting for his country, and is doing the best he can. What good would it do you to humiliate him in the eyes of the Georgia people by court-martialing him, and besides, whom have you to put in his place? Nobody better. When I find a situation like this, I take the officer into my tent and I talk to him there, and I try to see that at least he won't make the same mistake again." If an officer did make the same mistake, he might find himself transferred, with an extraordinarily kind letter, to the commissary department of West Texas.

Of necessity, as the war went on and his most experienced officers were lost, Lee was compelled to take more duties upon himself by calibrating, as required, the new officers' weaknesses and inexperience. But at the same time, Lee's trust in his foot soldiers remained undiminished. His veterans, he believed, would continue to "maintain themselves against the odds." Indeed, by this point in the war, with the heavy losses suffered among his front-leading generals (who as a proportion of total casualties, were twice as likely to be killed as a private), he thought the soldiers knew "their duties better than their general officers do and they have fought magnificently."

If Lee took on more field responsibilities and delegated less, it was because duty demanded it. Fundamentally, his trust in his men was unshaken. And just as he shared the men's privations in camp, so too, when the need for leadership demanded it, would he share their dangers in the field.

Lee set his men to digging what biographer Clifford Dowdey has called "the most elaborate system of field fortifications then seen in world warfare," designing "what amounted to mobile forts." The first test for his fortified army would be at the Battle of Spotsylvania Court House. Twice, during the fierce fighting, Lee had to be restrained from charging into the fray. When it was over, the results for Grant were even worse than they had been in the Wilderness. He had lost another 18,000 men, out of numbers that had been reinforced to 111,000, while Lee suffered no more than 10,000 casualties out of a troop strength brought up to 63,000. At this rate, if Grant hoped to defeat Lee by attrition, he would have to sacrifice the entire current strength of the Army of the Potomac and raise another.

Grant's army continued its swing south, meeting Lee's at the Battle of North Anna River. Once more, Lee stymied Grant, halting the Union advance in one of Lee's most cleverly fought tactical engagements. But such tactical success brought Lee little solace. His undiagnosed heart disease hit him hard here, though he remained imperturbable under fire. In one incident, he was standing on a porch in front of a house drinking a glass of milk when a shell crashed through the roof; neither he nor the glass of milk moved an inch. But he was too weakened to follow up his parry of Grant with a counteroffensive. He said, "We must strike them a blow. We must not let them pass us again." But there was no officer, in Lee's absence, fit to strike.

The armies repeated their mirrored shifts to the south, confronting each other at Cold Harbor. Grant, frustrated at Lee's continual thwarting of his advance, decided to rely on the sheer weight of his two-to-one superiority in numbers to end this bloody minuet. He hurled his men into a straightforward charge against Lee's newly and hastily erected fortifications.

For Grant, at least in human terms, it was a terrible mistake. The Union soldiers ran into blistering musketry and artillery fire, blue uniforms falling in grotesque, bloody clumps. Grant ordered assault after assault, thinking he had shaken the rebels. In fact, he had only demoralized his own men. The Battle of Cold Harbor was a Union disaster. Federal casualties were 10,000 men to Confederate losses of 4,000 men. While Grant's steady stream of reinforcements kept his army above 100,000 troops, it was *his* men who were wondering how long this could go on and *his* officers who feared political reaction to the staggering bill in casualties. In a month's worth of fighting, Grant had lost 50,000 men. Nearly 1,700 Federal soldiers had sacrificed their lives every day in Grant's war of attrition.

Because of Grant's reinforcements, the odds confronting Lee had not changed. Lee felt compelled, nevertheless, to divide his army in order to bring relief to the people of the Shenandoah Valley. He took advantage of the sudden quiet on his front after Cold Harbor to dispatch Jubal A. Early's corps to drive the Federals out of the breadbasket of the Confederacy. Old Jube, in a remarkable counterthrust, did exactly that, going so far as to strike into Maryland, causing panic in the Federal capital that he might be so crazy as to throw his troopers at Washington, D.C.

In the meantime, Lee had only 28,000 men, a provocatively small number to dangle in front of General Grant. But Grant had no interest in refighting Cold Harbor and had given up trying to find a way around Lee to Richmond. Instead, he opted to lay siege to Petersburg and cut Richmond's supply lines to the south.

Lee had foreseen this probability, but was powerless to prevent it. He also knew what it meant for the Confederacy. As he confessed to Jubal A. Early, if Grant were to cross the James River and attack Petersburg, "It will become a siege, and then it will be a mere question of time."

Lee would have to buy that time.

LEE'S LESSONS

• A leader who earns the respect of his adversary can save himself battles—as Lee did after Gettysburg.

• A leader should always conduct himself so that he might enjoy the "satisfaction that proceeds from the consciousness of duty faithfully performed."

• A leader seizes the opportunities of the day—*carpe diem.*

• A leader knows when to put himself on the front line to inspire his people.

• A leader does his own reconnaissance—there is no substitute for knowing the ground or for knowing the realities of the marketplace.

♦ A leader treats subordinates kindly if they try their best and fail. There is nothing to be gained by humiliating or oppressing subordinates. A leader's responsibility is to find suitable positions for his less experienced, less talented, or simply worn out junior officers.

CHAPTER NINE

HANGING ON

A SIEGE MEANT THAT Grant's war of attrition would be ratcheted up a notch, and that the challenge for Lee was all the greater. The Confederate commander had to defend Petersburg while still maintaining his freedom of movement. If Grant with his superior numbers could pin Lee down at Petersburg and then maneuver around him and attack Richmond directly, all was lost.

Lee was confronted with an extraordinarily difficult task. Still, his defense was largely successful, occupying Grant for nearly ten months, during which time the Union general could spare no men for an attack on Richmond. But if this delaying action could be counted as a victory, it was certainly a Pyrrhic one, because it was also during these ten months of successful defense that Lee witnessed the rest of the Confederacy wither, put to the torch by the swarming blue-coated foe who increasingly rode and marched with impunity over the people of the South.

Grant's initial assault on the defenses around Petersburg in June 1864 led to another bruising engagement, where the Union troops suffered so grievously, despite their overwhelming numbers, that the Union's offensive had to be cut short.

In Meade's words, "the moral condition of the army" was shattered.

Indeed, the Union troops had suffered such horrible casualties over the long struggle against Lee's army that their offensive spirit was drained to its dregs. A comfortable siege was what suited the Army of the Potomac. If Lee's men were hard-pressed, the Federals' spirit was incomparably lower than that of the Army of Northern Virginia. As Union General M. R. Patterson wrote, the Army of the Potomac "is nearly demoralized and the cavalry is no better than a band of robbers," preferring to inflict raids on civilians rather than fight Lee's rebel army. In the first two months of the siege, the Confederates, somewhat to their surprise, collected 8,000 Union prisoners, who felt well out of the fighting.

As the siege wore on, with Federal artillery shelling the city, Lee offered his wife a humorous assessment of the situation. "Grant," he wrote, "seems so pleased with his present position that I fear he will never move again."

However morally exhausted Grant's men, his was not an inactive siege. He continued to press and probe Lee's army. At its greatest extent, Lee's line of trenches stretched for nearly 55 miles.

In the most spectacular incident of the siege, blue-clad Pennsylvania coal miners burrowed beneath the Confederate lines, packed the tunnel with 8,000 pounds of explosives, and on July 30, 1864, detonated it. The blast tore a hole in the Confederate line, the earth collapsing into an enormous crater. The Federals poured into the breach. But with amazing sangfroid—amid the earth-shattering explosion that sent men flying and plunging to their deaths; in the choking, blinding smoke, dust, and dirt; with the Federals charging straight at them—the Confederates reformed around the lip of the crater, held their position in hand-to-hand combat, and opened fire on the Federals who had charged into the pit.

The Battle of the Crater cost the Union another 4,000 casualties to fewer than 1,300 casualties for the Confederates. Worse than that, from the Union perspective, was the speed with which the Confederates restored their lines. There was no chance to follow up with another attack on the breach. General Grant was appalled. "It was the saddest affair I have witnessed in the war. Such an opportunity for carrying fortifications I have never seen and do not expect again to have."

The Battle of the Crater looked like an act of Union desperation; the repulse, another blow to Federal morale. But Grant kept his men in place, and the siege dragged on through the winter and into the spring of 1865. The Union's noose was tightening around Lee. Atlanta, the anchor of the Confederacy's retreating western front, had been taken by the Federals the previous fall. Since then, the rest of the South had been reeling under the Union's terrible swift sword and purging torch. Virginia was the South's only remaining defensible front, the Army of Northern Virginia carrying the hopes and prayers—the very fate—of the entire Confederacy.

So desperate was the South's situation that there was a movement in Richmond to remove President Davis from office. What we need, said some, is a military dictator. Lee was their choice. But the idea was repugnant to Lee. He was fighting for the old Republic, not for power, and certainly not to become a Cromwellian Lord Protector. Without his support, the movement faded, but the pressure remained on Davis to shed some of his authority. On February 6, 1865, Davis tossed a sop to the critics who had accused him—in modern terms—of Jimmy Carter–like, self-defeating micromanagement. Davis named Lee the Confederacy's "General-in-Chief."

The title meant nothing to Lee, and he would rarely exert whatever additional nominal powers it granted him. Indeed, one of the few instances where it came into play was in Lee's insistence on reappointing General Joseph E. Johnston to command of an army. Typically, Lee thought nothing of Johnston's personal jealousy of him. He also overrode what he knew would be President Davis's objections. Davis had, after all, removed Johnston from command during the Atlanta campaign, when Johnston, as usual, seemed more adept at retreating than anything else. Lee wanted Johnston to command in North Carolina because Lee needed professional officers—and he needed men like Johnston, whose popular reputation remained high, and whose presence on the battlefield would support Confederate morale. That Johnston's reappointment was made on Lee's authority alone was made manifest by Davis's order, which noted that it was done "in the hope that General Johnston's soldierly qualities may be made serviceable to his country when acting under General Lee's orders, and that in his new position those defects which I found manifested by him when serving as an independent commander will be remedied by the control of the general-in-chief."

Think for a moment about this situation, and what it says about Lee's extraordinary position of leadership. How often do presidents—the ultimate commanders-in-chief, especially when as martially minded as Davis (Theodore Roosevelt, in this regard, would be a good parallel)—sack generals and then reappoint them on the advice of a military adviser? The answer is, of course, practically never. But Lee's new title was less about the power to appoint generals or about exerting authority in other theaters than it was a reflection of a new reality: the War Between the States had become Lee's war. For Southern troops, President Davis was a distant abstraction; Lee was the one man on whom all their hopes rested.

As Lee's aide Colonel Marshall recorded: "Such was the love and veneration of the men for him that they came to look upon the cause as General Lee's cause, and they fought for it because they loved him. To them he represented cause, country, and all."

Lee continually rode among his men, encouraging them, waving them into position when breaches were threatened. The men had little to eat: handfuls of cornmeal, perhaps a wad of what the troops called "Nausea Bacon," which one recalled could be chewed "for a long time, and the longer you chewed it the bigger it got. Then, by a desperate effort, you would gulp it down. Out of sight, out of mind." Another old soldier "thanked God I had a backbone for my stomach to lean up against."

Just as bad was the shortage of copper and lead for ammunition. Confederate soldiers on the line at Petersburg were limited to using 18 percussion caps a day, while Union soldiers were *required* to fire 100 rounds every day.

Shelby Foote notes that during the siege: "Lee's veterans fought less . . . for a cause than they did for a tradition. And if, in the past six months, this had become a tradition not so much of victory as of undefeat, it had nonetheless been strengthened by the recent overland campaign and now was being sustained by the current stalemate, which was all that Grant's hundred thousand casualties had earned him in this latest On-to-Richmond effort, launched in May. Mainly, though, Lee's veterans fought for Lee, or at any rate for the pride they felt when they watched him ride among them."

One observer who felt that pride noted of Lee at this period that his "countenance seldom, if ever, exhibited the least traces of anxiety, but was firm, hopeful, and encouraged those around him in the belief that he was still confident of success. . . . It must have been the sense of having done his whole duty, and expended upon the cause every energy of his being, which enabled him to meet the approaching catastrophe with a calmness which seemed to those around him almost sublime."

Lee's men responded to that example of sublimating self, of devotion to duty. Yet they never hoped to achieve the caliber of character exemplified by Lee. It was this inspirational cast of Lee's steady temper, his moral virtue, and his obvious inner strength that helped Lee get the utmost from his men.

Still, in his heart, Lee knew, as he wrote to President Davis, that the army could not hold the line at Petersburg indefinitely: "The inequality is too great."

One of Lee's recommendations for addressing this inequality was to arm freed slaves for the service of the South. Writing to President Davis, he noted that if the South ended slavery itself, it could "devise the means of alleviating the evil consequences to both races. I think, therefore, we must decide whether slavery shall be extinguished by our enemies and the slaves used against us, or use them ourselves at the risk of the effects which may be produced upon our social institutions. My own opinion is that we should employ them without delay. I believe that with proper regulation they can be made efficient soldiers."

Lee's argument for inducting slaves, under a "plan of gradual and general emancipation," into the Confederate armed forces was based, obviously, on dire necessity. But it also underlined that for him, the preservation of slavery was *not* the crucial Southern issue. Indeed, abolishing slavery could be turned to positive good for the Confederate cause.

Just as Lee had raised his sword in defense of his family, his friends, his heritage, and his state, would not black Virginians, who had helped raise white children, who as children themselves had often grown up with and played with white boys and girls, defend their own homes and defend the families they served against the Federal invader? Lee, whose own personal experience of slavery was limited, thought the answer would be yes. His belief was never tested—when the Confederate Congress finally capitulated to his advice and that of likeminded officers, it was too late. Certainly the thought of the

South arming its black population struck no fear in Northern hearts. As Abraham Lincoln said, "There is one thing about the Negro's fighting for the rebels which we can know as well as they can, and that is that they cannot at the same time fight in their armies and stay home and make bread for them. And this being known and remembered, we can have but little concern whether they become soldiers or not."

Lincoln had put his finger on the really crucial issue, which was food. The South's agricultural economy had been blockaded, burned, and derailed. In the trenches at Petersburg, while the Federals ate and drank their fill, Lee found it increasingly hard to scrounge supplies for his besieged men from denuded Virginia farms and warehouses. The harsh winter had been difficult enough. But the spring brought no new source of supply. Even worse, it brought an end to Jubal A. Early's efforts to keep the Shenandoah Valley in Confederate hands. His worn troopers, divided and outnumbered, were beaten by Phil Sheridan, who could now turn his attention to Lee.

Lee's own force numbered 35,000 men, roughly one-fourth of Grant's strength. Lee recognized that time's sands had virtually drained for the Confederacy. Lee's feelings toward the Confederate Congress veered on contempt. "Congress," he said laconically, "did not seem to appreciate the situation." In Richmond, he reported the stark facts to President Davis. Of Davis, Lee tried to cast a positive light on decisions he thought were manifestly misguided, speaking of Davis's "remarkable faith" in the prospect of ultimate victory, of his being "pertinacious in opinion and purpose," of his "unconquerable will power." But Grant's mighty host was growing stronger daily, while Lee's lines were stretched to the breaking point, and his men's food reserves were almost completely exhausted. Presidential willpower would not be enough to sustain them.

Still, Davis made a shocking concession to Lee's presentation of fact: Petersburg and Richmond would have to be abandoned. Lee's army, Davis conceded, would have to be freed to maneuver so that it could feed itself and attempt to unite with Joseph E. Johnston's fragment of an army in North Carolina.

It was a desperate strategy compounded by enormous tactical difficulties. For just how was Lee to disengage from the siege, on lines that stretched more than fifty miles, pursued by a giant, well-equipped adversary, and then race his army— with its skeletal horses and hungry men on the verge of collapse—to find Johnston in North Carolina?

He would have to fight his way out and somehow manage to keep Grant from turning his flank. Lee held the line protecting Petersburg and Richmond as long as he could, keeping the Federals back with occasional offensive maneuvers. But Grant knew that Lee's lines were paper thin, and on April 2, 1865, the Federals punched through. Lee could only stall him now. He could not defeat him here, and he could not hold him. Lee dictated a dispatch to the Secretary of War. "I see no prospect of doing more than holding our position here till night. I am not certain that I can do that. If I can I shall withdraw north of the Appomattox, and, if possible, it will be better to withdraw the whole line tonight from the James River." Petersburg and Richmond were lost to the enemy.

The Confederate army—and Lee in his headquarters— was now under continuous bombardment. Lee and his staff mounted their horses, the fire intensifying. As they rode away, their abandoned headquarters exploded under a rain of Union shells, the artillery bursts chasing after them. Lee angrily faced the hostile guns, his cheeks flushed. He would not be chased out of Petersburg. He would withdraw, and then bring his armies together where they could be revictualed to fight again. There was no sign of panic. As Colonel Taylor noted, Lee "was self-contained and serene" and "acted as one who was undisturbed by the adverse conditions in which he found himself."

The Army of Northern Virginia that left Petersburg numbered no more than 30,000 men. Lee's plan was to march them to Amelia Court House, where he expected to find supplies. As the troops arrived, one observer recorded that they were "still in good spirits...of excellent morale...and nowhere could be seen a particle of gloom." That assessment might be overly sentimental and roseate, but the fact is, the army still could not imagine defeat under the command of "Marse Robert." If anything, the soldiers felt relieved to escape the trenches of Petersburg.

But then Lee's hopes, and his men's, were quickly crushed. At the railroad station at Amelia Court House, Lee found trains loaded with inedible cannon balls. The food he expected had been sent everywhere but here—to Danville, Virginia, to Lynchburg, Virginia, to Greensboro, North Carolina. The cannonballs, on the other hand, were worthless to Lee, save to break the backbones of his already weakened supply horses.

The food his men needed was now long marches away. The situation was turning from desperate to hopeless. He sent a message to Danville, the nearest of the supply dumps on his route to North Carolina, ordering that rations be sent to the railroad station at Jetersville, Virginia, eight miles south of Amelia Court House. He dispatched supply wagons to scour the countryside for whatever else might be available from friendly farmers.

But nothing was to be had, and Federal cavalry under Phil Sheridan were riding to seize Jetersville.

Lee had slipped through Grant's fingers, but it would not be long before the Federal army was upon him. Now came a bizarre reenactment of the Lee versus Grant campaign of 1864, with Lee maneuvering continuously to the west as

Grant had maneuvered south, trying to find a clear road to North Carolina, as Grant had probed for a way to Richmond. Grant's troops shadowed Lee, meeting him at every turn. Where in the 1864 campaign Lee had checked Grant with bloody repulses at the end of every arcing movement, here the Union cavalry pressed the pursuit, keeping the Confederates on the move while maintaining, in Shelby Foote's words, "a respectful distance." But there were also bloody engagements, the worst of which was at Sayler's Creek. The tides of fortune had shifted so dramatically that now it was the starving, straggling, ragamuffin Army of Northern Virginia that suffered hugely disproportionate casualties. At Sayler's Creek, the Confederates were again outnumbered more than two to one, but their casualties were on the order of *seven to one,* including the loss of eight captured Confederate generals, among their number Dick Ewell and Lee's son Custis.

When Lee saw the survivors from Sayler's Creek fleeing to join his part of the army, he exclaimed, "My God, has the army been dissolved?"

The answer came from General William Mahone: "No, General, here are troops ready to do their duty."

"Yes, General, there are some true men left." Lee raised a gauntleted hand and pointed to a mass of blue horsemen forming on the horizon. "Will you please keep those people back."

Mahone set off, and Lee proceeded to assist him, seizing a battle flag and riding amid the broken Confederates, urging them to rally. His eyes picking a general out of the mob, Lee said, "General, take these stragglers to the rear, out of the way of Mahone's troops." Lee's brown eyes hardened. "I wish to fight here."

Mahone screened the Confederate retreat, while Lee reassembled his forces. The united Army of Northern Virginia now numbered about 15,000 men, with approximately

80,000 troops under Grant in pursuit. Lee knew that he could not hope to outrun the Union commander. His only option would be to try and fight again. But the end for Lee was apparent on April 9, 1865. It was then that General John B. Gordon—a Georgian elevated by Lee to corps command during the siege at Petersburg, and who had proved himself an able subordinate—fought the last engagement of the Army of Northern Virginia near Appomattox Court House. "Tell General Lee," Gordon ordered, "I have fought my corps to a frazzle, and I fear I can do nothing unless I am heavily supported by General Longstreet's corps." General Longstreet—who had returned to duty at Petersburg—anchored Lee's other flank. If Lee moved him to support Gordon, there would be nothing between Union General Andrew Humphreys's wing of the Federal army and Lee's headquarters.

When Lee received this message, he said, "Then there is nothing left me but to go and see General Grant, and I would rather die a thousand deaths."

Lee sat down on a log with his young artillery officer, E. P. Alexander, who had directed the batteries at Gettysburg. Lee asked Alexander's opinion of the army's circumstances. Alexander was "wound up to a pitch of feeling I could scarcely control" and recommended that the army should "scatter like rabbits and partridges in the woods" and fight a guerrilla war.

Lee shook his head and replied: "Suppose I should take your suggestion and order the army to disperse and make their way to their homes. The men would have no rations and they would be under no discipline. They are already demoralized by four years of war. They would have to plunder and rob to procure subsistence. The country would be full of lawless bands in every part, and a state of society would ensue from which it would take the country years to recover. Then the enemy's cavalry would pursue in the hopes of catching the principal officers, and wherever they went there would be fresh rapine and destruction." Then, somewhat humorously, Lee added: "And as for myself, while you young men might afford to go to bushwhacking, the only proper and dignified course for me would be to surrender myself and take the consequences of my actions."

Lee reminded Alexander that they could not think of what surrender would cost them personally in terms of lost honor; they had to do what was best for their country. Alexander later recounted, "I had not a single word to say in reply. He had answered my suggestion from a plane so far above it that I was ashamed of having made it."

Until now, Lee had been no more willing to surrender than Alexander. Only two days before, Lee had seen his son Rooney lead a cavalry countercharge against the Federals. It was a gallant, successful action in the old style of Jeb Stuart. "Keep your command together and in good spirits, General," Lee told his son. "Don't let them think of surrender. I will get you out of this." As long as there was a flicker of hope for a conventional victory, Lee would keep it cupped in his hands. But now the flame was extinguished.

Lee's despair was evident when he was overheard saying, "How easily I could get rid of all this and be at rest. I have only to ride along the line and all will be over. But it is our duty to live. What will become of the women and children of the South if we are not here to protect them?"

As always for Lee, there was a higher responsibility than self. At Appomattox that responsibility meant surrender of his army. Lee believed in the restraints of conventional warfare. The horrors of war, he thought, were bad enough; there was no need to make them worse. And for him, guerrilla war offered only anarchy and an even more terrible spilling of violence into the lives of civilians. It meant more Sheridans and Shermans and reprisals and hangings. It meant more destruction of farms and cities, more suffering for innocent noncombatants, more weeping women, more suffering children. By all civilized standards, Lee believed a true leader would have to swallow his pride and say no to a partisan campaign. Surrender is hateful, but a leader must count the cost not just to himself but to his people.

If Lee felt any bitterness—and he did—it was reserved for the fire-eaters in the Confederate Congress who had spoken of blood and iron while avoiding combat themselves, and who treated the needs of his army as an afterthought. Late in the siege at Petersburg, Lee had told his son Custis, "I have been up to see the Congress and they do not seem to be able to do anything except to eat peanuts and chew tobacco, while my army is starving. . . . Mr. Custis, when this war began, I was opposed to it, bitterly opposed to it, and I told these people that, unless every man should do his whole duty, they would repent it; and now: they—will—repent."

But it was not Congress that would have to face General Grant, it was Lee. On Palm Sunday, April 9, 1865, General Robert E. Lee dressed in a bright, clean uniform with a sword, red sash, and highly polished boots. "I have probably to be General Grant's prisoner," he told one of his officers by way of explanation, "and thought I must make my best appearance."

However jocular the quip, Lee was still not entirely reconciled to accepting the bitter cup of surrender. For the last two days, Lee and Grant had been exchanging notes across the lines, discussing the possibility. Longstreet had been stalwart throughout. On the evening of April 6, Lee had received a message from Grant, saying that the "results of the last week must convince you of the hopelessness of further resistance on the part of the Army of Northern Virginia in this struggle." Lee read the note and passed it to Longstreet without comment. Longstreet read it and said, "Not yet." Lee agreed.

Now Longstreet told his commander, "Unless he offers us honorable terms, come back and let us fight it out." Lee seemed inspirited by his "old war horse." Longstreet remembered that "the thought of another round seemed to brace" Lee, who mounted Traveller for one of the greatest set-pieces in American history.

SURRENDER

It would be enacted at the Appomattox house of Wilmer McLean, formerly a resident of Manassas. McLean had fled Manassas, and the war, after his house was struck by an artillery shell in First Manassas in 1861. Now, ironically, his house would close the war in a meeting between the immaculately dressed Virginian aristocrat and the mud-spattered soldier from Ohio, Ulysses S. Grant.

Grant later recorded that Lee "was a man of much dignity, with an impassable face. . . . Whatever his feelings, they were entirely concealed from my observation; but my own feelings, which had been quite jubilant on the receipt of his letter [agreeing to discuss terms for the surrender of the Army of Northern Virginia], were sad and depressed. I felt like anything rather than rejoicing at the downfall of a foe who had fought so long and valiantly, and had suffered so much for a cause, though that cause was, I believe, one of the worst for which a people ever fought."

Grant's view of Lee marked one of the most telling aspects of Lee's character as a leader. Though Lee had come to represent the Southern cause—a cause that many Northerners regarded not only as wrong but as morally evil, requiring the punishing scourge of Reconstruction—Lee, by the time of his death, had become a tragic hero for the South *and* the North, an *American* hero of unsullied motives and character.

Grant attempted small talk, but Lee preferred that the matter be settled, the scene not drawn out. Lee asked Grant to commit his terms to writing, which Grant did with the same concision that marked Lincoln's Gettysburg Address, in fewer than two hundred words.

Lee read them. Until now he had been stiff and cold. But Grant's straightforward simplicity, honesty, and fairness compelled Lee to say, "This will have a very happy effect on my army." He made only one suggestion, that Grant make a provision for the men to keep their horses, which belonged to them personally and not to the army. Grant refused to alter the terms, but assured Lee that he would instruct the Union officers charged with accepting the surrender and with arranging the Confederates' parole to allow any man who owned a horse or mule in service to keep it.

Lee thanked Grant and said, "This will have the very best possible effect on the men. It will be very gratifying, and will do much toward conciliating our people." As copies were made and Lee's letter of acceptance prepared, Lee told Grant that he had a number of Union prisoners that needed to be exchanged as quickly as possible, "for I have no provisions for them. I have, indeed, nothing for my own men."

"Suppose I send over 25,000 rations. Do you think that will be a sufficient supply?"

It was more than Lee could have hoped for, and he thanked Grant for his generosity.

When the conference ended, Lee shook hands with Grant, bowed to the other officers, and stepped outside, replacing his hat and returning Union salutes. His anguish expressed itself briefly. While his face remained impassive, he absentmindedly balled one of his gauntleted hands into a fist and punched it into a receiving gauntleted palm: once, twice, three times. Then, joined by his two staff officers, he remounted Traveller and rode away, returning Federal salutes by raising his hat.

The dignity of the scene was somewhat ruined, at least for Wilmer McLean, when Union officers bargained with each other for possession of McLean's chairs, tables, anything that had been used in the surrender or that had merely been in the same room with Grant and Lee. To satisfy everyone, furniture was broken up, the pieces divided as spoils.

While this went on behind his back, Grant returned to his headquarters and informed his staff: "The war is over. The rebels are our countrymen again."

In Lee's camp, he was greeted with Rebel Yells, as though he were a chieftain returning to his braves. Their spirits were high, but they had to ask the inevitable, if unbelievable, question. "General, are we surrendered?"

His answer came: "Men, we have fought the war together, and I have done the best I could for you. You will all be paroled and go to your homes until exchanged." Then, after a pause, "Good-bye."

"General, we'll fight 'em yet. Say the word and we'll go in and fight 'em yet."

Lee shook his head sadly, and rode Traveller through the gathering throng.

"I love you just as well as ever, General Lee!" The men, dirty and hungry, patted Traveller's flanks, and reached up to shake their commander's hand.

"Farewell, General Lee. I wish for your sake and mine that every damned Yankee on earth was sunk ten miles in hell!"

It was an un-Lee-like sentiment, but what leader of any organization would not feel gratitude for having inspired such service and spirit? Had it been asked to, the Army of Northern Virginia would have fought to the last man. If its men had outlasted their ammunition they would have charged like banshees with bayonets—and all for one cause, all for one man: a man they loved rather than feared, a patriarch they trusted as they would trust their own fathers and as they would expect to be trusted by their own sons.

Ultimately, after being ground down in four years of unequal combat, they were surrounded in southside Virginia. Just the night before, they had marked the camps of the various Union forces glittering around them like a reflection of fire on a ring of steel. In plain fact, Grant's strategy of attrition had worked. The men in the Army of Northern Virginia had no hope of reinforcements. They "were whipped," as Shelby Foote has noted, "about as thoroughly as any American force had ever been or ever would be, short of annihilation, but it was part of their particular pride that they would never admit it, even to themselves."

It was a tribute to Robert E. Lee's leadership that they had that pride. Under his leadership they had fought so well, had endured so much, and were willing to go on enduring until death claimed them. They had become one of the most extraordinary fighting forces in military history, and for that the credit belongs to General Robert E. Lee.

The enemies of the Army of Northern Virginia certainly accorded the Confederate force every respect. At Appomattox, Union Colonel Charles S. Wainwright wrote, "The Army of Northern Virginia under Lee . . . today . . . has surrendered. During three long and hard-fought campaigns it has withstood every effort of the Army of the Potomac; now at the commencement of the fourth, it is obliged to succumb without even one great pitched battle. Could the war have been closed with such a battle as Gettysburg, it would have been more glorious for us. . . . As it is, the rebellion has been worn out rather than suppressed."

In reporting news of his surrender to President Davis, Lee noted that the "enemy was more than five times our numbers. If we could have forced our way one day longer it would have been at a great sacrifice of life; at its end, I did not see how a surrender could have been avoided. We had no subsistence for man or horse, and it could not be gathered in the country . . . the men deprived of food and sleep for many days, were worn out and exhausted."

Knowing that Davis might contemplate, like the young artillery officer E. P. Alexander, fighting a guerrilla war rather than giving up the cause of the Confederacy, Lee counseled the president that a "partisan war may be continued, and hostilities protracted, causing individual suffering and the devastation of the country, but I see no prospect by that means of achieving a separate independence. . . . To save useless effusion of blood, I would recommend measures be taken for suspension of hostilities and the restoration of peace."

Lee the soldier accepted the verdict of the battlefield. Davis the politician could not. In flight from Richmond, he attempted to carry on the struggle, encouraging Joseph E. Johnston to race with him to Texas, where the battle could be renewed. Johnston ignored him and surrendered shortly after Lee. As word of the surrender drifted through the South, other commanders stacked their arms and surrendered. Some sent themselves into exile in Mexico, Brazil, or the western territories of the United States.

President Davis was eventually captured and imprisoned. But there was no formal end of the Confederate States of America. Davis's flight, in the words of Clifford Dowdey, had "robbed the Confederacy of the opportunity to terminate its career with the dignity which Lee had salvaged for his own army."

Yes, that is true. But insofar as Lee was, for the people of the South, the true embodiment of their cause, their honor was intact. The war was over, and it ended, in the imagination of everyone, North and South, not with the capture of a desperate president fleeing with his wife, or in the horrible crime of political murder committed at Ford's Theater, but with the meeting of two men, each alive with the best characteristics of his respective section of a divided land, who could shake hands as officers and gentlemen with mutual respect and a care for their people and posterity. In his surrender, as much as in his greatest victories, Lee showed the true measure of a leader.

LEE'S LESSONS

◆ A leader must keep hope alive when his people must work—even suffer—under the most adverse conditions, and continue to seek every opportunity for victory.

◆ A leader must recognize that, in the end, there are worse things even than defeat. When facts dictate that one's business has failed, or that one's war is lost, and that no further effort could possibly achieve success, a leader knows it is far better to face facts squarely than to carry on a struggle that results only in needless effusions of red ink or red blood, of reputations or lives destroyed. Ultimately, a leader must count the costs of sacrifice not only to himself but to his people and act accordingly.

CHAPTER TEN

LEE, THE TEACHER

Between the Mexican War and the War Between the States, Lee had been superintendent at West Point, and he returned to education after the war, when he accepted the offer of a small college in Lexington, Virginia, to become its president. It was then called Washington College, and is now Washington and Lee University, the home of Lee Chapel, and the burial site of Lee's horse Traveller. Adjacent, across a field of grass, is the Virginia Military Institute, the school where Stonewall Jackson had taught, and where lie the bones of his mount, Little Sorrel.

Until Lee was offered the post of president of the college, he had been unsure how he would earn his living. Again, as when he had managed Arlington plantation, he hoped for a quiet, agricultural life, though his dreams were even more humble now than in the past. "I am looking for some quiet little house in the woods where I can procure shelter and my daily bread," he wrote, adding the telling phrase, "if permitted by the victor."

While General Grant had been magnanimous at Appomattox, it was an open question how the conquering Federals would treat the Southern states—especially after the assassination of Abraham Lincoln, one of the worst of the calamities to befall the South, which Lee, with his longstanding horror of violence against civilians, considered "a crime previously unknown in this country, and one that must be deprecated by every American."

Standing on the side of reconciliation was Lincoln's vice president, now president, Andrew Johnson. As vice president—though a Democrat and a Southerner—Johnson had been on the side of the radicals in Congress who had advocated harsh treatment of the South. But now, faced with the responsibility of uniting the devastated Southern states with their brethren in the North, he adopted Lincoln's more lenient position. Even so, Johnson was, understandably, not popular in the South, and Southerners professed to see very little evidence of his newfound "moderation."

In the Congress of the United States, Johnson was almost equally unpopular. Arrayed against him were his former allies, the radical Republicans, who wanted to punish the South, strip every former Confederate of the rights of citizenship, hang a few of the more famous rebels, and essentially turn the South into a radical Republican fiefdom. The radicals' political opponents in the South would be unable to vote and the newly enfranchised blacks would be beholden to the radicals. As such, the South would be open for the radicals to plunder and "reconstruct" as they saw fit. If there was any opposition, martial law could be enforced with draconian severity. In fact, under the Reconstruction regime, proud Virginia, which had been governed by an elected legislature since the 17th century and was the home of more American presidents than any other state—including the founders, Washington, Jefferson, Madison, and Monroe—would become Military District Number One, occupied territory under an imposed military governor.

Such was the temper of the times that there were those in Congress who thought the John Brown strategy of encouraging a slave insurrection against white Southerners was not outdated. Perhaps if the blacks slew "one-half of their oppressors" that would teach the remaining Southern whites just who was in charge now. Such was the vision expressed by Senator Benjamin Wade of Ohio in a letter to Senator Charles Sumner of Massachusetts.

Even the British novelist Anthony Trollope—who, from afar, was a staunch supporter of the Unionist cause—said of Reconstruction, "Never has there been a more terrible condition imposed upon a fallen people." It was imposed upon a people who had already suffered as no Americans ever had or, by the Grace of God, ever will again. *One-quarter* of the draft-age white male population of the South lay dead from battle or disease. In material terms, as historian Gary Gallagher notes, the war "cost the Confederacy two-thirds of its assessed wealth . . . killed 40 percent of its livestock, destroyed more than half its farm machinery, and left levees, railroads, bridges, industry, and other parts of the economic infrastructure"—not to mention entire cities—"severely damaged or ruined." The South was prostrate, and "Reconstruction" was the conqueror's heel on its throat.

Nevertheless, from the first moments after his surrender at Appomattox, Lee had pressed upon his former soldiers, and upon those who sought his advice, the need to make the best of their new lives in the Union and to rebuild their devastated homes, farms, towns, and cities. There was constructive work enough for everyone in the South; there was no need to continue hopeless partisan warfare or inflame already heated passions. To his former aide Colonel Walter Taylor, Lee wrote that he should encourage their veterans to "set to work, and if they cannot do what they prefer, do what they can." Every former Confederate soldier was now needed as a laborer to restore Virginia's prosperity, "to sustain and recuperate her."

To Mosby's Rangers, who were willing to fight on in Virginia, Lee said: "Go home, all you boys who fought with me, and help build up the shattered fortunes of our old state."

Lee himself, however, still faced the possibility of being tried for treason. In this grim setting, Lee was offered an escape. Virginia-born Matthew Fontaine Maury—the father of oceanography, as well as a scientist, naval officer, and engineer who had helped the Confederates experiment with torpedoes—invited Lee to join a Confederate colony in Mexico.

Lee thanked Maury for his letter and admitted that Mexico offered some advantages—he had fond memories of it—but he could not in good conscience take his leave of Virginia: "The thought of abandoning the country and all that must be left in it is abhorrent to my feelings, and I prefer to struggle for its restoration and share its fate, rather than to give up all as lost."

As he had at the outbreak of the war, Lee took his stand with Virginia. There was no doubt that this was what his duty required, even if it meant that he, like Jefferson Davis, might find himself in chains in a Union prison—or even hanged. "Now, more than at any other time, Virginia and every other state in the South needs us," Lee said. "We must try and, with as little delay as possible, go to work to build up their prosperity." As for himself, Lee was unconcerned, saying wryly, "It matters little what they may do to me. I am old and have but a short time to live anyhow."

In the five years between the end of the war and his death, Lee was offered many profitable business ventures, all of which he turned down because he judged that none of them required him to do useful work, but were merely efforts by others to capitalize on his name. The only business opportunity he accepted in the final years of his life was serving on the board of a prospective Valley Railroad Company. This he did because it promised a necessary rail link between Lexington, the home of Washington College, and the rest of Virginia. As Lee once told a traveler seeking the best road to his new home town, "It makes but little difference, for whichever route you select, you will wish you had taken the other." The board convinced him that without his assistance, there was little chance the necessary capital could be raised. Even with his assistance, Lee felt he had joined a somewhat Quixotic venture. When he was asked to become president of the company shortly before his death, Lee accepted, but reluctantly. "It seems to me," he wrote, "that I have already led enough forlorn hopes."

Others had higher aspirations for him, including political office. Despite his being barred from voting (his American citizenship was not restored until 1975), Lee was considered as a possible gubernatorial candidate (following in the footsteps of his father and fulfilling his wife's wishes) and even as a possible presidential candidate. For the latter office, he was endorsed by the *New York Herald,* which counseled the Democratic Party that if it had any hope of electing a former general who could defeat Republican Ulysses S. Grant in the coming election, it should "nominate General R. E. Lee . . . making no palaver or apology. He is a better soldier than any of those they have thought upon and a greater man. He is one in whom the military genius of this nation finds its fullest development. Here the inequality will be in favor of the Democrats for this soldier, with a handful of men whom he moulded into an army, baffled our greater Northern armies for four years; and when opposed by Grant was only worn down by that solid strategy of stupidity that accomplishes its object by mere weight."

Flattering words, though Lee, if he read them, was doubtless unmoved. He quietly demurred every time his name came forward for political ends. In fact, he avoided talking of politics—or the war—whenever he could. He did this not because he had no political thoughts or interests or because he was ashamed of his years as a Confederate, but because he thought anything he said publicly might be misappropriated and used to stir up the old war fever, hindering the South's efforts to rebuild itself. His counsel for his people was simply work—work for your families, work for your home state, and work at a Christ-like tolerance for any and all abuse that came from carpetbaggers and vengeful authorities from the North.

When pressed on his political beliefs, Lee would tell people that he had no difficulty accepting the abolition of slavery, by law—indeed he took great comfort and solace from the warm greetings he received from blacks after the war—but that he also believed Southerners who served the Confederacy deserved the same rights as any other citizens, and that if he could vote, he would do so for "the most conservative eligible candidates for Congress and the legislature," candidates who believed in the old republic of sovereign states and the limited powers granted the federal government by the Constitution.

Though he was disinclined to speak of the war, Lee could be sparked to equally adamant statements defending the years he spent in the saddle for the Confederacy. When a friend of Lee's told him he was working exceedingly hard in his civilian job because he was "so impatient to make up for the time I lost in the army," Lee upbraided him immediately. "Mr. Humphreys," Lee said, "however long you live and whatever you accomplish, you will find that the time you spent in the Confederate army was the most profitably spent portion of your life. Never again speak of having lost time in the army."

It seems obvious in retrospect that after the war Lee would turn his mind to educating the young men of the South. But at the time, it was not so clear. Though he had been superintendent at West Point, he did not consider himself a qualified educator, and indeed, he had then preferred service as an officer in the field rather than as a desk-bound administrator at the military academy.

Moreover, when, in the summer of 1865, he was offered the post of president of Washington College, Lee felt obligated to draw the college's attention to two unhappy facts. First, he had to concede that he was physically less able than he had been, and though he might be able to handle the responsibilities of administration, he would unlikely have enough strength to teach as well. Perhaps more important:

> Being excluded from the terms of amnesty in the proclamation of the President of the U.S. . . . and an object of censure to a portion of the Country, I have thought it probable that my occupation of the position of President might draw upon the College a feeling of hostility . . . I think it the duty of every citizen . . . to do all in his power to aid in the restoration of peace and harmony. . . . It is particularly incumbent on those charged with the instruction of the young to set an example of submission to authority, and I could not consent to be the cause of animadversion upon the College.

But there was no denying that in his heart, the post offered him a role he thought he should fulfill, that met his desire to do something for his state, that met his prayer that he might be spared "to accomplish something useful for the good of mankind and the glory of God." He closed his letter to the college by adding that should the board "take a different view, and think that my services . . . will be advantageous to the College and Country, I will yield to your judgement and accept it."

The college board, which had been stunned by its own presumption in offering Lee the post, rushed to assure him that they could think of no happier outcome for the school than for Lee to become its president.

TEACHING LEADERSHIP

Lee's years as president of Washington College offer a fasci-
nating portrait of his ideas about leadership—refined after
years of war, reflecting his lifetime's experience, and directed
particularly at teaching others to be leaders.

The post was no sinecure—or at least, he did not approach it that way. He was an active president, reshaping the
school to meet the new ends he designed for it. As his biographer Douglas Southall Freeman notes, he took a "college that
had been very near to death" and made it "live again with a
vigor it had never known." Charles Bracelen Flood, in his
book *Lee: The Last Years,* goes even further, writing, "By the
time he died . . . Robert E. Lee was entitled to a position in
the first rank of American educators, without reference to his
military past."

As Lee had had to build an army for a new country at the
start of the War Between the States, so too would he have to
make a new college out of the remnants of what remained of
the old. Lee's son Robert E. Lee Jr. recalled that Washington
College's "buildings, library, and apparatus had suffered from
the sack and plunder of hostile soldiers. Its invested funds,
owing to the general impoverishment throughout the land,
were for the time being rendered unproductive and their ultimate value was most uncertain. Four professors still remained
on duty, and there were about forty students, mainly from the
country around Lexington. . . . It was very poor, indifferently
equipped with buildings, and with no means in sight to improve its condition."

Lee oversaw new construction and a massively expanded
fundraising effort, while, with his usual abhorrence of waste
and debt, he kept the school's accounts balanced. He revital-
ized the college by adding new departments that took the
classical ideals of the old school—a curriculum that focused

on Greek, Latin, and the traditional literary canon—and admixed them with what he saw as the practical training the young men of the South would require in the work of rebuilding their society. The new courses included engineering, farming, commerce, modern languages, law, and other fields, even a new department of journalism—perhaps a pet hobby horse of one unimpressed, except by its capacity for mischief, by the quality of reporting he had seen during the war.

Lee took a backwater college and made it a university—today one of the most prestigious private universities in the nation. Before he died, Lee was planning to add even more new courses, including departments of astronomy and medicine. As an active soldier, Lee had had little time for outside reading—aside from newspapers, which he read eagerly, and the Bible, of which he was a loyal student—through most of his career. The one exception was when he was superintendent of West Point, when he made frequent use of the library, but mostly to purposive ends: he prepared himself for the day when he might be less of an engineer and more of a commanding officer by reading French military history, especially the campaigns of Napoleon and the work of Swiss strategist Baron Henri Jomini. Now, however, Lee's vision had broadened, and he conducted his own renaissance at Washington College.

But the vast expansion of courses he oversaw was not Lee's main goal at the school. "My only object," he said of his students, "is to endeavor to make them see their true interest, to teach them to labor diligently for their improvement, and to prepare themselves for the great work of life." Lee believed that in preparing students for "the great work of life," education must impart knowledge and skills. Hence, the new "practical" courses he included in the curriculum. But these were meaningless if a young man was not taught to govern himself. Just as he had sought officers capable of self-command, so too did he seek to inculcate self-command in his students. He did this not by forcing them to recite lengthy catechisms but by giving them freedom and holding them accountable for their actions. In essence, he taught them to swim by throwing them in the water.

As a general, Lee had relied heavily and purposefully on the initiative of his subordinate officers in executing his plans and adapting them to the shifting tides of battle. As an educator, Lee similarly believed that students needed to govern themselves.

It is important to understand, however, that he was by no means an anarchist, trusting to the students to behave well on their own. Lee was a great believer in subordinating oneself to lawful authority. He would say over and over again, in different variations, that "obedience to lawful authority is the foundation of manly character." Denying oneself—and denying the overly indulgent dictates of an eagerly forgiving ego— was a key to doing what was right, and the reason why deference to lawful authority was an essential check and duty.

But while Lee believed in subordinating oneself to lawful, received authority, he also believed that a man stood or fell on his own. Like his fellow Virginian Thomas Jefferson, he believed that the government that governed least governed best: it encouraged individuals, through experience if nothing else, to make responsible use of freedom because they bore the costs.

He did not believe in excuses for bad behavior. Miscreants generally deserved forgiveness, but only if they conceded that what they had done was wrong, not if they tried to explain it away. Nor did he believe in allowing individuals to shelter themselves behind a lawyerly parsing of rules supported by reams of accompanying paperwork, which was intended only to clutter and confuse, or behind a bureaucracy of attenuated responsibility. He had no time for blame-shifting or what amounted to *collective irresponsibility*—typified for him by the Confederate Congress. Most of all, he did not believe in a proliferation of laws and regulations that by necessity could not all be enforced, and as a consequence bred "dead letters" that inspired only "disrespect for the whole body of laws."

Lee believed, with Charles Dickens, that the law could be an ass. While he could be as strict a disciplinarian and enforcer of the law as anyone, he did not believe in the blind application of legal precedent. He believed that the individual and his circumstances must always be taken into account. As Lee said, "I always respect persons and have little care for precedent." Lee did not believe that rules should be applied with Procrustean ferocity, that one size, as it were, would fit all. So he kept the strict rules of the school to a minimum. As Lee said of Washington College under his administration: "We have no printed rules. We have but one rule here, and it is that every student must be a gentleman." The practical definition of a gentleman, for the purposes of the school administration, was someone who would abide by a self-governing honor code, which Lee introduced to Washington College.

Lee's principle was this: *the good leader teaches responsibility by giving it to others.* Perhaps the most compelling testimony of Lee's belief in granting liberty to subordinates— within the confines of simple rules—was his abolition of compulsory chapel.

To modern agnostic sensibilities this action might seem unremarkable. But that is to miss the point entirely. For Lee was not a modern agnostic, but a devoted Episcopalian, active in church affairs. He himself attended chapel every morning. Building a new chapel was his top construction priority for the school. He once said, "If I could only know that all the young men in the college were good Christians, I should have nothing more to desire. I dread the thought of any student going away from college without becoming a sincere

Christian." Moreover, Lee submitted the name of every student to the local clergyman of that student's religious affiliation, and encouraged that clergyman to look after the spiritual instruction of his young sheep.

The key issue for Lee, and for Lee's method of leadership, was that however worthy the end—and presumably no end can be more important than a divine one—compulsion was not the way to achieve it. *A true leader does not rely on force, but on the power of example.*

In Lee's own words: "As a general principle you should not *force* young men to do their duty, but let them do it voluntarily and thereby develop their characters." He had believed that throughout his career. As superintendent at West Point he had noted, "Young men must not expect to escape contact with evil, but must learn not to be contaminated by it. That virtue is worth but little that requires constant watching and removal from temptation."

Lee's counsel that young men needed to be taught to govern themselves was something he believed applied to everyone: from the youngest students—that is, children—to his own highly diversified student body with its scarred, hardened veterans of the war. A leader needs to exact obedience, it is true, but neither "harshness nor violence should ever be used" except in extraordinary—generally criminal—cases, as when Lee ordered executions for desertion in the face of the enemy.

Lee's rule for governing students was the same as for Lee's officers in governing their men—to control others, a man must first show that he can control himself. And by controlling himself a leader teaches the greater lesson of self-denial and the concomitant rule that however dissimilar are individuals' "characters, intellects, and situations, the great duty of life is the same, the promotion of the happiness and welfare of our fellow men."

If this sounds overly idealistic, in practice at Washington College, it proved effective. It became a point of pride for the students to abide by the honor code and to work to do their best. The men obeyed Lee, according to one student, "not because they feared but loved him, and I don't think there was one of the boys . . . but would have died defending him if necessary." As noted before, General Lee turned Machiavelli's principle that "it is better to be feared than to be loved" on its head and showed that the reverse could be true. For a business leader, the lesson might very well be the same, remembering always that in a free market, labor is free to move but is less likely to do so where tied by bonds of affection, loyalty, and devotion to a common cause.

Lee could be strict indeed with issues of economy—acting, in essence, as financial overseer of his student charges. He knew that in the impoverished South, virtually every student at Washington College was there at great financial sacrifice to his family. Because he respected those who paid the bills, Lee refused to abide idleness—or wasteful drunkenness—from his students. He expected his students to carry a heavy course load and endeavored to find them work in the summer so that they could help pay their own way. Just as students should be taught, and expected, to govern themselves, so too, Lee believed, should they be taught the virtues and the rigors of financial independence.

But as much as Lee was respected, loved, and admired, the inevitable question arose one day from a sophomore called into his office. Lee took the student aside and told him that he must apply himself more to his studies, that only hard work would guarantee him success in life.

"But, general," the sophomore replied, citing Lee's own history, "you failed."

Lee neither scowled nor grew sharp with the youngster, but said simply, "I hope that you may be more fortunate than I."

Lee knew that, as he wrote a friend, "we failed, but in the good providence of God apparent failure often proves a blessing."

It has often been said that however great a commander Lee was in the field, his greatest service to his nation was his example after defeat. Douglas Southall Freeman, for one, illustrated how Lee's "gospel of silence and goodwill, of patience and hard work" helped bind the wounds of the nation.

This is true. But Lee taught an even deeper lesson to those with whom he had direct contact, his students and friends. It was this: one must do one's duty to the best of one's ability, whatever the cost, whatever the consequences, and trust that Providence will turn everything, even apparent disaster, to some useful purpose, however dimly perceived, if it can be perceived at all.

It would be profoundly wrong to conclude that Lee, with his trust in God's merciful providence, was untroubled by defeat. For Lee felt the woes of the South with terrible force. Many after the war commented on the ineradicable sorrow in his face. It was as if he carried the tragedy of his region on himself. But Lee knew that he had done all that he could do. He had performed his duty the best that he could. The verdict of battle had been settled, and now, as in everything else in life, it was his duty to make the best of circumstances, and making the best of things meant not self-gratification but finding ways to help others.

This was the responsibility he tried to instill in his students. As collegians they were an elite. They were being groomed for positions of power in the various professions and the various tasks desperately needed by their prostrate society. Lee's students were to be trained to execute their role as leaders—as self-governing, self-denying gentlemen.

Lee's description of what a gentleman should be was Lee's description of what a leader should be. He summarized the goal when he wrote:

The forbearing use of power does not only form the touch-stone, but the manner in which an individual enjoys certain advantages over others is the test of a true gentleman.

The power which the strong have over the weak, the magistrate over the citizen, the employer over the employed, the educated over the unlettered, the experienced over the confiding, even the clever over the silly—the forbearing or inoffensive use of all this power or authority, or the total absence of it when the case admits it, will show the gentleman in plain light. The gentleman does not needlessly or unnecessarily remind an offender of a wrong he may have committed against him. He can not only forgive, he can forget; and he strives for that nobleness of self and mildness of character which impart sufficient strength to let the past be the past.

A true gentleman of honor feels humbled himself when he cannot help humbling others.

One doubts that they teach this at the Harvard Business School.

Indeed, it would seem that for many of today's leaders success is measured by the exultant use of power, whether financial, administrative, or otherwise. The goal is self-fulfillment, and the means to reach that end are advertising, trumpeting, employing, or enforcing every advantage one has over one's fellows.

This was not Lee's way, because Lee did not believe in self-fulfillment and took no pleasure in the use of force. If Lee had ever taught a course on leadership at Washington College, he would undoubtedly have told his students what he told the young mother seeking his blessing for her infant son: "Teach him he must deny himself." A leader's job is to serve.

This ideal of service has immediate, practical, daily applications for any leader. As Lee's wartime aide Walter Taylor noted:

I had excellent opportunities at that time to observe General Lee as a worker, and I can say that I have never known a man more thorough and painstaking in all that he undertook. Early at his office, punctual in meeting all engagements, methodical to an extreme in his way of despatching business, giving close attention to details—but not, as is sometimes the concomitant if not the result of this trait, neglectful of the more important matters dependent upon his decision—he seemed to address himself to the accomplishment of every task that devolved upon him in a conscientious and deliberate way, as if he himself was directly accountable to some higher power for the manner in which he performed his duty. I then discovered, too, that characteristic of him that always marked his intercourse and relations with his fellow men—scrupulous consideration for the feelings and interests of others; the more humble the station of one from whom he received appeal or request, the more he appeared to desire to meet the demand if possible or, if impracticable, to make denial in the most considerate way, as if done with reluctance and regret.

To lead is to serve, if for no other reason than that every leader should conduct himself as though his work, no matter how secular, is in the service of God. Moreover, as in the Gospels, the rule of leadership is that to *whom much is given, much is expected,* and a leader must do what he can for those less well placed than himself.

As far as a leader's expectations of others, Lee might have taught future leaders to demand much but expect inevitable human failure, and discipline subordinates accordingly. Lee always demanded much of his generals and soldiers in what he asked them to achieve on the battlefield, just as he demanded much of his students in the time they would allot to their studies, and in the self-governing, self-disciplined com-

portment he required of them. In both cases he was richly re-
warded with high morale and high performance.

But he also knew that his students were young and high-
spirited, and would, or at least some of them would, inevitably
run afoul academically or otherwise. Lee was generally indulgent of these failings, as long as the student did not exhibit bad
intent or character, in which case the student might be dismissed. Lee's reproofs were usually given so considerately that
they were even described as "motherly." Students, in fact,
were often surprised at how mildly they were treated. But Lee
exacted from these sessions such a bond with his pupils that
most were eager never to disappoint the old man again.

Just as a general must allow for "the fog of war" to bring
what the Prussian military theorist Karl von Clausewitz called
"friction" to the best-laid plans, so too, Lee believed, must an
academic leader allow for youth to express itself. Similarly, a
business leader must understand the inevitable stresses and
other sources of "friction" under which his employees operate. Lee would advise a leader to set ambitious goals for his
subordinates, but to be understanding if, after every conceivable effort, they fall short.

Lee would also have taught his future leaders to grant
subordinates as much autonomy as possible. Just as "virtue is
worth but little that requires constant watching and removal
from temptation," so too are employees worth but little if
they cannot be trusted to work and find ways to improve
their work, to innovate, on their own. A leader should lift the
obstacles blocking his employees' success. He should not
follow the example of the Soviet army and assign a commis-
sar to every unit to enforce ideological discipline and shoot
the wayward.

Lee would have taught that a leader who leads by force or
threats or who creates dissension and conflict is a leader who

has failed. Although he was a supremely aggressive commander who sought always to bring his enemy to combat, one
must remember that before secession, during the war in squabbles among his subordinate commanders, after the war, and
certainly in his personal relationships, Lee was opposed to
conflict, sought to avoid it, and acted always as a peacemaker.
He would have echoed the Gospels and told his students of
leadership that blessed are the peacemakers, for that is the role
of a gentleman focused not on himself and the achievement of
his own desires but on some higher goal of behavior and common good. Making peace is a leader's responsibility and something that comes from his rising above the squabbling and
selfish belligerence of man's nature.

When Lee said that it is well that war is so terrible or we
should grow too fond of it, this is what he meant: war, as history has taught us, is sometimes inevitable, even necessary.
But we must not let the use of force, or for that matter the
necessary if harsh actions of business—and the principles or
arts that must animate them—override the higher claims of
our nature and of right in our other affairs, or when force can
be avoided even in the affairs that require it.

War, as Clausewitz famously defined it, is the continuance
of politics by other means. In the politics of a free people, the
first goal, Lee would say, is peace with honor, persuasion
through debate, not settlement by force of arms. But when
force of arms is chosen, a commander should behave like Lee—
audacious, aggressive, and combative in strategy (though not
in personal manner), and responsible in the use of power (including having a mindfulness for his opponent's civilians and
their rights and privileges).

In business, too, the striving for competitive advantage,
the "hype" of marketing, the focus on man as a narrowly materialistic being with appetites and attitudes to be stimulated,
prodded, and flattered—all these things might be necessary,

and within their own sphere even positive goods, in that they manufacture and spread wealth, but they are not the whole of humanity, or even the best part, or even helpful to the best part. A business leader might take his cue from Lee and find it useful to remind himself that it is well for us to know that an executive's power over his staff, the cut and thrust of competition, the "collateral damage" of products that serve amoral or immoral ends, the Mammon that is the marketplace, can all be so terrible so that we should not grow too fond of it at the expense of our families, our neighborhoods, our greater communities—our states, our country—or our religion.

More prosaically, Lee would have instructed his future leaders to slash red tape, noting that paper regulations—and their embodiment in a bureaucracy—are an enemy of effective leadership and a promoter of collective irresponsibility. A leader should work to have as few rules encumbering his administration as possible, and stick to them. To quote Lee, "We must make no heedless rules. We must never make a rule that we cannot enforce." Just as Lee was opposed to rules becoming meaningless by there being too many of them, so should business leaders eliminate excessive and unnecessary rules that only breed employee cynicism and even contempt for the officious bureaucrats who try to uphold them.

Lee would have taught that in judging subordinates, a leader should be generous, but once a decision is made, he should stick to it and enforce it with vigor, speed, and finality. As superintendent, Lee was so solicitous of his cadets at West Point that the stern then-Secretary of War Jefferson Davis thought he worried about them too much, and later wrote that "it was perceptible that his sympathy with the young people was rather an impediment than a qualification for the superintendency." But though Lee treated the progress of every cadet with the utmost concern and consideration and believed in treating each cadet as an individual with individual circumstances, he never sought to lower academic standards for the benefit of the failing or to excuse bad behavior. When discipline was meted out, or resignation encouraged, or dismissal enforced, it was performed as justice should be, swiftly and surely, with no doubts. In one instance, Lee received a student in his office to go over his disciplinary reports. The student had a wad of tobacco in his mouth. Lee ordered him to "Go out and remove that quid, and never appear before me again chewing tobacco." When the boy returned, the plug still in place, Lee wrote him a note. The young man was thereby immediately "dismissed from Washington College for disrespect to the President." Lee would not allow a contumacious streak to grow in a student or allow a bad example to contaminate the student body. As Lee wrote of student punishment, "When it is necessary, true kindness requires it should be applied with a firm hand, and not converted into a reward." Once a decision was made, he stuck to it. Lee never supported a dismissed student's being readmitted or being allowed to resit examinations for reentry to the school.

Finally, Lee would have taught his students of leadership to remember the character of their people. Just as Lee was a careful judge of the character of his officers, so too did he take care to know his students. He knew every student's name and every student's academic strengths and weaknesses.

But at the same time, he was not overly familiar with his students. He kept a dignified distance and adopted the manner he had throughout his military career of being with the men, but not of the men. He did not pretend to a back-slapping, chummy intimacy that he did not own. His restraint and seriousness won respect. His quiet concern won affection and devotion.

And there is one other point to be remembered here, and that is Lee's expectations of his subordinates and his method of leadership were both grounded profoundly in his heritage as a Virginian, as an American linked directly to America's founders, and as a familial descendant from the England of the Magna Carta. Lee's rules of leadership are rules for leading a free and self-governing people.

Lee's ideal was freedom. His prescription was self-discipline. His method was kindness. When a professor complained of the slowness of some of his pupils, Lee replied, "May I give you a piece of advice, sir? . . . Always observe the stage-driver's rule. . . . Always take care of the poor horses."

For Lee, taking care of the poor horses, the troubled students, and the ragged soldiers who proudly called themselves "Lee's Miserables" was what leadership was all about.

Lee's health was never certain after the war. He knew that death was stalking him. On September 28, 1870, Lee was departing his office when a student approached with a small portrait of the general that a young girl had wanted Lee to autograph. The student said he would be happy to come again later, as Lee was obviously off to his next appointment. But Lee replied, with more than mere generosity, for he knew his time was short, "No, I will go and do it now."

It was the last time Lee would enter his office.

That afternoon, Lee walked through the rain to attend a vestry meeting. When he returned home, he sat with his family at the dinner table. He bowed his head to say grace, but no words came. He sat back in his chair, erect as a soldier on parade. He could not speak.

In this, his final illness, his speech eventually returned, though he said little. His fading strength allowed him only monosyllables, except when fever took him. Even then the phrases were brief. He was back in the war. "Tell Hill he must come up!" he said suddenly and clearly.

Lee met his last trial with the same composure and dignity that he had met every other challenge in his life. He did not rage against the night, but treated death as inevitable and even as a release. In the desperate final days of the war, when Lee was brought the news that General A. P. Hill had fallen, tears came to his eyes, and he said, "He is now at rest, and we who are left are the ones to suffer." On October 12, 1870, Lee's own suffering ended. His final words were recorded as "Strike the tent," a phrase he had uttered countless times on his long campaigns in defense of Virginia.

But while Lee's tent was struck on this day for the final time, history has shown that Lee's place in the hearts and minds of his countrymen has never been struck—not in the devastation of defeat, nor during the bitter recriminations of Reconstruction, nor at any time for the near century and a half since the end of the War Between the States.

For Americans, Lee remains an ever-available tutor—as he was, by example, for his students—in the lessons of service, devotion to duty, and leadership.

LEE'S LESSONS

• The true measure of a leader is how well he matches effective fulfillment of his duty with the forbearing use of force.

• A leader remembers that the goal of leadership is not self-fulfillment but service to his fellow men.

• A leader demands much but expects inevitable human failure, and disciplines subordinates accordingly, with generous regard for their best efforts.

• A leader grants subordinates as much autonomy as possible; subordinates who cannot be trusted should not be employed.

• A leader has as few rules encumbering his administration as possible—and sticks to them, always bearing individual circumstances in mind.

• A leader should remember Lee's most famous dictum, and its corollaries: "It is well that war is so terrible; we should grow too fond of it."

CHAPTER ELEVEN

THE MARBLE MAN

W HEN HIS ELDEST SON was at West Point, Lee wrote
him a letter of fatherly advice and instruction. He counseled,
among other things, that:

> You must study to be frank with the world: frankness is the
> child of honesty and courage. Say just what you mean to do
> on every occasion, and take it for granted that you mean to do
> right. If a friend asks a favour, you should grant it, if reason-
> able; if not, tell him plainly why you cannot: you will wrong
> him and yourself by equivocation of any kind. Never do a
> wrong thing to make a friend or keep one; the man who re-
> quires you to do so is dearly purchased at a sacrifice. Deal
> kindly, but firmly, with all your classmates; you will find it the
> policy which wears best. Above all, do not appear to others
> what you are not. If you have any fault to find with any one,
> tell him, not others, of what you complain; there is no more
> dangerous experiment than that of undertaking to be one
> thing before a man's face and another behind his back. We
> should live so as to say and do nothing to the injury of any
> one. It is not only best as a matter of principle, but it is the
> path to peace and honour. . . .

> Duty, then, is the sublimest word in our language. Do your
> duty in all things. .... You cannot do more, you should never
> wish to do less.

Worthy advice—all of it—for any prospective leader, or for anyone for that matter. As a fatherly prescription it might seem unremarkable, except that today doubtless few fathers would feel comfortable saying such things—thinking them either irrelevant or clichés at best, humbug at worst. Today, a collegian with truly up-to-date, hip American parents would more likely be advised to use a condom when indulging in what in Lee's day was regarded as the sin of fornication.

This is no flippant comparison, but something that strikes to the core of Lee's example of leadership. Clifford Dowdey, one of Lee's best biographers, and Douglas Southall Freeman, his Pulitzer Prize–winning chronicler, both concluded that Lee's was a simple Christian soul, one of little interest to Dr. Sigmund Freud. He was the sort of man who could not only utter the sentiments in this letter with all due sincerity and no hint of self-consciousness, but who followed them in his own life.

Lee was a man who saw the necessity of rising above a material or corporeal existence, a goal far less commonplace in our own times, except perhaps as a vague, undisciplined, and even self-centered longing for our lives to have an eternal or spiritual value.

For Lee and for many of his contemporaries, this was no vague longing—and selfishness had nothing to do with it. One's life was simply, obviously, where principle became flesh; it was the place for heroic action, for self-sacrifice, for the making of mighty vows. The spiritual, if one may call it that, was not something to be put off as dreamy bedtime reading, it was something to be lived, its demands executed.

As Dowdey says, Lee "assumes heroic stature because he was a product of an age in which men held heroic concepts of life and its meaning."

If Lee's path seems in some ways the road of perfection, he is different from modern Americans only in that he thought that road was worth attempting, disciplined himself for the task, and did it. Controlling his temper, for example, was not something that came entirely naturally to him. It was a matter of conscious self-management that was betrayed only by the red that would rise in his face and neck, and the clipped, sometimes curt, manner he would adopt when angry. Lee was a man of forceful passions. One need only look at his constant audacious efforts to bring the Union army to combat, his riding to the front of his troops in the heat of battle, his gauntleted fist punching his open hand. It was an act of will, the embodiment of training, the fulfillment of his desire for self-command that helped Lee keep his passions in check.

It is easy to see why, for the religion-drenched Southerners, Lee quickly came to be regarded as a Christlike figure. Theirs was not the celebrity worship we are used to today, but the response of a deeply religious people who knew *The Pilgrim's Progress* and who saw in Lee a striver—for his God and for his country, his Virginia and his Southland. They saw a man who rejected temptation and vanity fair, who suffered terribly but who never wavered from his determination to do what was right.

If this seems too much an uncomfortable and unacceptable counsel of sainthood for modern Americans, we should remember that while Lee was not lax with himself, he had a sense of noblesse oblige that moderated his expectations of others. Without any sense of personal arrogance, Lee accepted human imperfection, the inevitability of foul-ups and failure to which humanity is prone, the ineluctable fact that dreams always fall short of reality. Indeed, Lee knew—as a Christian—that everyone is in constant need of forgiveness and that no one should be sparing in forgiving others; and he did not except himself from the need for forgiveness or the obligation to forgive. In his after-battle reports Lee assumed that every officer had tried his best and that if an officer had failed or made mistakes, his errors were the product of well-meaning intention. It was only when he saw an officer as having been derelict in his duty—as when, near the end of the war, General Pickett left his troops to attend a shad bake—that Lee might growl a rebuke, and in Pickett's case, dismiss an officer as being unworthy of sharing arms with the Army of Northern Virginia (this incident underscores that even during the desperate final days, when every man counted, Lee was intent on maintaining the discipline of his army).

Lee was someone who believed that abstract principle was not the final word on anything. Duty, he believed in, yes. But duty directed one to serve *people,* not *principles.* Lee's attachment to what was tangible and real—to the soil of Virginia, to his family, friends, and neighbors in the Old Dominion—goes far to explain his loyalty to the South in the War Between the States. Lee would not consent to raising a sword—or having others raise a sword—against his own people. If the slaves were to be made free, as he hoped they would be, that process should be achieved through moral persuasion and free legal debate, not by force. The principle of freeing the slaves, like the principle of maintaining the Union, was not one that he could accept as being so superior that it could be imposed by violence. It did not trump the bond between himself and his fellow Virginians and Southerners, or his belief that force was a hateful expedient, however desirable the end. As he once wrote his son Custis, "I am opposed to the theory of doing wrong that good may come of it. I hold to the belief that you must act right whatever the consequences."

Though Lee would likely quibble with these words of George Orwell, they do, in part, apply to him, and help explain why Lee, despite some images to the contrary, is among the most human and the least cold and distant of commanders: "The essence of being human is that one does not seek perfection, that one *is* sometimes willing to commit sins for the sake of loyalty, that one does not push asceticism [or perhaps political principle] to the point where it makes friendly intercourse impossible, and that one is prepared to be broken up by life, which is the inevitable price of fastening one's love upon other human individuals."

When one looks at photographs and paintings of him, one can see how Lee "was broken up by life." One sees first the dashingly handsome young soldier, clean-shaven except for long sideburns, just turned 31 in 1838; then, in the early 1850s, a dark-haired, moustached, fatherly Lee, in apparently comfortable middle age. By 1862, the war well under way, one sees, with shock, a bearded man, his hair and whiskers turned entirely white; yet his eyes remain kindly, giving him a grandfatherly appearance. By 1863 and 1864, his countenance, at full length, looks slightly weary, perhaps annoyed at the trouble of being photographed, but in portrait, the face remains pleasant. In 1865, shortly after his surrender, Lee posed for the most famous photographer of the war, Matthew Brady. Lee still looks the perfect image of a grandfather, but one that no child would want to cross. The eyes look as hard as flint, the face resolute. If any photos capture Lee the warrior, Brady's do.

Finally, there are two famous photographs of Lee at Lexington. The first, taken in 1866, shows him mounted on Traveller, still looking like a Confederate warrior chieftain. The other, taken the year of his death, shows a man in formal dress, preternaturally old, his hair and beard like coarse cotton.

But in focusing on the precipitate physical decline charted by these photos, one might give too much weight to the obvious tragedy of Lee's life. There was much more to him than that. The historian Emory Thomas in his brilliant biography of the general has captured much of Lee's complexity as a man. While cast in a heroic mold, while dedicated to Christian self-denial and self-control, while being the aggressive, combative warrior trying to find a way to "get at those people," Lee was someone who "resisted the temptation to take himself seriously and developed a comic vision of life . . . alive to the absurdities of the human condition."

Lee expressed a dry, occasionally sardonic, humor with male friends and colleagues. As a son of the courtly South, he had a deep vein of flattering, even mildly flirtatious, humor for women. Perhaps most revealing of all, he was playful and indulgent with children, for whom he was never too busy. Throughout the war, he corresponded with young admirers. British military historian Francis Lawley was so impressed by what he saw of Lee's natural affinity for children that he felt obliged to echo the Christological language of the South: "If it may be said without irreverence, it was impossible at such moments to forget the affection with which the Master, whom General Lee loved to serve, 'suffered little children' to draw near unto His presence, and saw in them an image of that childlike faith which is the shortest and surest path to the kingdom of heaven." In one charming postwar incident, Lee, as president of Washington College, remained seated during the graduation ceremonies, contrary to protocol, so as not to disturb a five-year-old who had climbed into his lap and fallen asleep.

With his own children, Lee practiced what he preached—disavowing the use of force and encouraging emulation by example. For Lee's children, this proved a generally successful strategy, as they held him in such awe that they never dreamt of contradicting him. But he could be exacting. Lee, the stern-visaged paterfamilias, always demanded a *quid pro quo* if his children wished to have him read them a story. He demanded they tickle his feet. No tickling, no story.

A winsome example of Lee's playfulness that remained even after his children were grown comes from his days in Lexington, when he once received in the mail a gift of an afghan and a tea cozy. The old general threw the afghan around his shoulders, perched the cozy on his head, and danced to a tune his adult daughter Mildred played on the piano.

Lee's humor, as this last example might illustrate, was part of his being the great anti-egotist. Lee had no need for the ancient Roman tradition of a conquering general, parading his captives through the streets in triumph, being followed by a slave whose job was to remind him that all fame is fleeting. For Lee not only knew that instinctively, he never thought of fame at all. As Confederate Vice President Alexander Stephens said of Lee, "he remained unspoiled by praise and success." He never sought adulation and applause and never considered that he deserved them.

Lee merely executed his duty to the best of his ability and gave no thought to anything else. In this, his biographers Clifford Dowdey and Douglas Southall Freeman are certainly right: Lee's method of life was simple. But it was also based on a profound and traditional Christian paradox. Lee saw personal freedom as something that came from and was fulfilled by service to God. One finds freedom by obeying the commandments, just as one retains freedom by obeying the law. It is sin that forges the shackles of passion and compulsion that deny freedom, just as unlawfulness can lead to incarceration.

So if a leader seeks freedom of action, he must first bind himself to the laws of God and man. For an example of how this principle worked itself out in Lee's life, remember how

General Joseph E. Johnston, a man with a high and prickly regard for himself, tried to avoid having President Jefferson Davis micromanage his operations. Johnston's method was simply to refuse to communicate with the president unless it suited him.

Lee, however, took a different approach. Lee, the anti-egotist, the man bound by a dutiful sense of the hierarchy of human affairs, gained much greater freedom under Jefferson Davis because he deferred to him and communicated with him as often and as helpfully as he could. Lee retained Davis's trust and was granted a plenitude of autonomy. In part, of course, this was because of Lee's undoubted competence in the field. But it was also because he was open with the president and left him in no doubt that he willingly accepted that Davis, as the elected civilian authority, was ultimately in charge.

Lee accepted the paradox that freedom came from deference and self-restraint because it was right by law, by good manners, and by what was required of a Christian gentleman. It also echoed the Gospels. Just as he who would save his life must lose it, he who seeks freedom of command—who seeks to lead—must subordinate himself to the proper authority in the ordained hierarchy of life.

If Lee respected the rights of his superiors, he also respected his subordinates. For one thing, he treated them like adults. His method of leadership was far removed from the childish ersatz challenges and rewards contemporary managers like to dangle before their employees—selecting managers-of-the-month, gathering self-conscious "team" cheerleading sessions, organizing weekend whitewater rafting or mountain climbing to teach "leadership" and "teamwork." It is hard to think of anything more removed from Lee's natural dignity and respect for his men and his officers.

In any enterprise worthy of the name there should be challenge and inspiration enough. And it is well to remember that a business, or any similar organization, is not a "family" (and it is obnoxious when it pretends to be); it is not an organic, primary, ineradicable, and holistic bond of loyalty. It is, rather, driven by a specific goal. A business should be what the Army of Northern Virginia was: a "voluntary association of gentlemen organized for the sole purpose" of one's enterprise. That purpose is best achieved, and one's subordinates are best inspired, by *doing*, not by playing games and offering carnival prizes.

Lee motivated his men by riding the lines and encouring them. He inspired his officers by giving them responsibility. He offered his example, and he offered his trust. Lee did not see his subordinates as tools on which to exercise his ego but as individuals with specific strengths and talents, whose ideas should be consulted (though not necessarily accepted) and whose freedom to respond to changing circumstances in the field, except where it might conflict with an overall plan, should be assured.

Part of Lee's anti-egotism was his supreme confidence, an inner security tied both to the promises of his religion—that a benign Providence would turn all things to good—and to the knowledge that he had unsparingly done his duty to achieve the goal set before him. As such, there was no room, no possibility, for a guilty conscience. He always did all that could be done, and rather than let himself become distracted by the multitude of potential disasters facing him and his army, Lee maintained a sense of calm and order—a hierarchy not only of command, but of priorities—focusing on the most pressing task, tackling challenges one at a time, and preferring whenever possible to take the battle to the enemy, to throw *him* off balance.

Lee never dwelt on the frailties of his own position, because he felt he could cope with any calamity. Anything that might befall him and his army was within God's plan. His job was to do the best that he could with the tools he had and under the conditions that God gave him. Any and all disappointments, he felt, should be accepted with resignation and with a resolve to make the best of circumstances.

As a college president, Lee would quote Marcus Aurelius: "Misfortune nobly borne is good fortune." It was a sentiment he held all his life.

During the war, noting depredations against Southern churches by Northern troops, he counseled his wife, "We must suffer patiently to the end, when all things will be made right."

After his surrender at Appomattox, he wrote a cousin-in-law, "We must be resigned to necessity, and submit ourselves in adversity to the will of a merciful God as cheerfully as in prosperity."

And during some of the worst throes of Reconstruction he reminded his son Rooney that duty demanded that all "earnestly work to extract what good we can out of the evil that now hangs over our dear land."

It was Lee's faith in God, his dutiful search for good in the bleakest of circumstances, and his extreme distaste for any complaining or repining that made him such a dedicatedly resilient personality, the perfect embodiment of Kipling's lines about the man who "can meet with triumph and disaster and treat those two imposters just the same."

Lee's resilience was not only a source of personal strength, it was an inspiration to others, and one of the means by which he brought a redemptive quality to human circumstances. In Lee's self-imposed task to take any situation God had given him and turn it to some good, he sometimes appeared to assume the mantle of another old soldier, St. Francis of Assisi.

Lee took great pleasure in nature, and was as solicitous about the needs of animals as he was about the needs of his men. Once, when under heavy shelling during the siege of Petersburg, Lee stopped and took time to return a baby sparrow to its nest. Amidst the shrapnel of war, Lee's action implied, at least something could be saved, some kindness done to the littlest and most harmless of things.

His sheer force of character, directed toward the preservation of peace and, if it is not too loaded a word, righteousness, was evident in one particularly memorable incident shortly after the war. During a service at St. Paul's Episcopal Church in Richmond, a black man rose to accept communion from the priest. In the words of one eyewitness, the effect of the black man's action "upon the communicants was startling, and for several moments they retained their seats in solemn silence and did not move." The priest himself was described as "embarrassed." But the tension was broken when Robert E. Lee went up the aisle and knelt beside the black man at the chancel rail. The others in the church followed, and the peace of St. Paul's was restored.

When Douglas Southall Freeman completed his four-volume biography of General Lee, he noted, "I have been fully repaid by being privileged to live, as it were, for more than a decade in the company of a great gentleman."

Every leader should strive to be remembered in such terms. General Robert E. Lee offers us an example of how to do so.

Vincit qui se vincit.

LEE'S LIEUTENANTS

STONEWALL JACKSON, LEE'S RIGHT ARM

Why does the South adore Stonewall Jackson? He was not an obviously lovable man, being rather plain in looks and harshly unbending in principle. He was certainly not a romantic, dashing cavalier like Jeb Stuart, a stainless aristocrat daring all odds like Robert E. Lee, or even a wizard of the saddle like Bedford Forrest. Yet at Stone Mountain, Georgia—the Confederacy's Mount Rushmore—it is Jackson who is memorialized with Lee and Jefferson Davis; Jackson, the odd, dour, stern Presbyterian; Jackson, the poor, orphaned boy from what is now West Virginia; Jackson, the man who became Lee's right arm.

Jackson triumphed because of a relentless self-discipline that helped him overcome a hard-scrabble childhood. Shy, stubbornly dutiful—working over and over to get things right—coolly wary of distractions, unswervingly and bluntly honest, he quickly alienated himself from the more easygoing, sociable, aristocratic Virginians at West Point.

In a region not short of eccentrics, Jackson stood out as an exceptional one. He was a food faddist and a hypochondriac, devoted to water cures, stale bread (he timed its aging with a watch), and an idiosyncratic exercise program. When he was a professor at the Virginia Military Institute, the cadets nicknamed him "Tom Fool" Jackson, regarding him as an occasional martinet (though they took advantage of his poor hearing—the price of his being a former artillery officer) and continual eccentric. Most striking to the cadets was his performance as an instructor, where he could have been mistaken for a flesh-covered automaton. Jackson painstakingly memorized his lectures, spending his evenings, when his eyes were too tired to read, staring at a wall, reciting the lectures in his head. In the classroom he was unable to deviate from their literal recitation. An unexpected question could set him repeating his lecture from the beginning.

Jackson was also known as a fiercely committed Christian, albeit one who, with typical eccentricity, more often than not fell asleep in church. Nevertheless, he was a sincere and pious Presbyterian, married to a minister's daughter (twice; he was once widowed), a student of theology, and the devoted sponsor and teacher of a black Sunday school that not only taught religion but skirted the law by teaching slaves and their children to read and write.

Nor was he, as some might expect, a particularly narrow man. As a young lieutenant, he had admired the women in Mexico, he liked to pepper his letters with Spanish words (he considered Spanish a more romantic language than English), and while thoroughly Protestant in his own faith, he never countenanced anti-Catholic bigotry. Indeed, while serving in Mexico and considering matters of faith, Jackson respectfully consulted with the Catholic Archbishop before he settled on joining the Presbyterian church. From that experience Jackson gained, in the words of an associate, "more tolerant views of popery than most zealous Protestants."

Had it not been for the War Between the States, Jackson might have been remembered as that not unknown phenomenon, the oddball professor, but also as a godly man, happiest when with his family, and as someone who had been a fearless young lieutenant in the Mexican War, almost recklessly cool under fire.

It was this last point, of course, that would impress the VMI cadets. Jackson could have told the boys of Lexington that the only time he remembered uttering a lie was in Mexico when, with bullets and shells bursting all around him—and in the dirt between his feet—he assured his men they were perfectly safe. He would have left it to others to remind his listeners that at war's end, as one of his colleagues noted, "No other officer in the whole army in Mexico was promoted so often for meritorious conduct or made so great a stride in rank."

War transformed Jackson. In it, his shaky health miraculously cured itself and his eyes glittered as action approached. In the War Between the States, Jackson, the stiff-minded scholar, drew his battered VMI kepi low over his eyes and became a brilliantly aggressive and audacious general, rising at "early dawn" (which by Jackson's watch could be 3:30 or earlier in the morning) and marching his men so rapidly, so far, so unpredictably that Stonewall's ragged infantry became known as his "foot cavalry."

But if Jackson's light burned most brightly in war, he, like so many other brave men who fought for the Old Dominion, prayed for peace. As an instructor at VMI, he had even come close to doubting the morality of war except in a defensive cause. As secessionist passions rose, Jackson, remembering his experiences in Mexico, wrote his wife saying: "People who are anxious to bring on war don't know what they are bargaining for; they don't see all the horrors that must accompany such an event."

Jackson, like Lee, did not want the Union torn asunder, but he also refused to abide by a Union that, in his view, was bent on trampling the Constitution, violating the rights of his home state, and subjugating the South by force.

When war came, Jackson's advice was "to draw the sword and throw away the scabbard." "We must give them no time to think," he said. "We must bewilder them and keep them bewildered. Our fighting must be sharp, impetuous, continuous. We cannot stand a long war." And to that end, he wanted to take the war to Northern territory to "force the people of the North to understand what it will cost them to hold the South in the Union at bayonet's point."

His thinking was in perfect alignment with Lee's, and it was Lee who first spotted the talented general in the Shenandoah Valley and who did all he could to support him. Lee recognized in Jackson an independent-minded commander capable of causing consternation to the Federals, drawing Union troops away from Richmond, and bringing victory in short, sharp, surprise engagements in the Valley, liberating Virginia's breadbasket and raising Southern morale when Confederate tidings elsewhere were grim.

Jackson's first string of successes came in what is known as the Valley campaign of February to June 1862. The sheer brilliance of the campaign has made it a continuous beacon to military strategists. Jackson, with a force of fewer than 16,000 men, managed to occupy the attention of four times that many Federal troops, to bewilder and bloody them—indeed to inflict nearly three times as many casualties as he took himself—and to provide a much-needed hero that suited the South's combative, impetuous spirit, that fulfilled its conceit that Southern boys could outfox any Yankees, and that when it came to fighting, one man in grey was worth four in blue.

Jackson's strict Calvinist religion—he was a stickler, for instance, for respecting the Sabbath, not even wanting to draw ammunition on a Sunday—only added to his luster. He was the South's avenging sword, the Christian soldier bending his knee to pray before chasing the Union invader from the Valley.

He was Lee's model lieutenant because—with the striking exception of his failure during the Seven Days campaign, when Lee took command to drive the Federals from the outskirts of Richmond, and Jackson appeared, disoriented and exhausted—he was a self-governing officer, unafraid of independent responsibility, eager to act, and fierce in combat.

Jackson's chief axiom of war was to find the weak point of the enemy, surprise him there, hit him hard, and when he runs, keep after him: "Always mystify, mislead, and surprise the enemy, if possible; and when you strike and overcome him, never let up in the pursuit so long as your men have strength to follow; for an army routed, if hotly pursued, becomes panic-stricken, and can then be destroyed by half their number. The other rule is, never fight against heavy odds, if by any possible maneuvering you can hurl your own force on only a part, and that the weakest part, of your enemy and crush it. Such tactics will win every time, and a small army may thus destroy a large one in detail, and repeated victory will make it invincible."

Lee appreciated Jackson's speed and aggressiveness. Personally, he warmed to Jackson. As a corps commander, Jackson became the perfect executor of Lee's vision.

But Jackson's method of leadership was very different from Lee's. Jackson demanded absolute secrecy and blind obedience, and got it by confiding in no one. His officers and troopers never knew where they were going, or how far they would march, or whether Jackson's circuitous routes were meant to mystify the enemy or themselves.

Lee, in his usual diplomatic way, tried to encourage Jackson to be more communicative with his brigade and division commanders, telling him, in one instance: "A. P. Hill you will find I think a good officer with whom you can consult and by advising with your division commanders as to your movements much trouble will be saved you in arranging details as they can act more intelligently."

Though Lee's letter had no effect on Jackson's conduct, Lee had accurately diagnosed the most serious flaw of Jackson's method of leadership. Although maintaining secrecy on the march was admirable, Jackson's subordinate officers were often forced to operate without knowing their objective, and that sometimes led to confusion. Moreover, their dependence on Jackson's orders kept them from taking the initiative when orders were lost, or in circumstances where Jackson had imperfect knowledge or was himself operating below par, as in his deadly inactivity during the Seven Days. Finally, the lack of communication between Jackson and his brigade commanders inevitably caused friction and paper affrays between himself and some of his more spirited officers, whom he had no qualms about putting under arrest.

General George Pickett summarized Jackson's critics when he quoted another officer's observations:

Old Jack holds himself as the god of war, giving short, sharp commands distinctly, rapidly and decisively, without consultation or explanation, and disregarding suggestions and remonstrances. Being himself absolutely fearless . . . he goes on his own hook, asking no advice and resenting interference. He places no value on human life, caring for nothing so much as fighting, unless it be praying. Illness, wounds, and all disabilities he defines as inefficiency and indications of a lack of patriotism. Suffering from insomnia, he often uses his men as a sedative, and when he can't sleep calls them up, marches them out a few miles; then marches them back. He never praises his men for gallantry, because it is their duty to be gallant and they do not deserve credit for doing their duty.

There is, frankly, much truth in that description. Jackson was a taskmaster, and could be unforgiving with subordinates, though he had lapses himself. He was also a poor judge of men, preferring to surround himself with parsons and favorites rather than with talented professionals.

But one cannot argue with Jackson's successes, or with the fact that the tight-lipped, hard-marching, stern-disciplined eccentric won the respect and admiration of his soldiers, who, as one trooper recalled, "unconsciously adapted some of the General's ways; they were terse and laconic with strangers, and the answer 'I don't know,' was often all they had to say. But their devotion was superb and their courage sublime."

Another of his dusty, hungry men recorded that "Every time he would pass our brigade we would all commence cheering him. . . . It got to be a common saying in the army, when any cheering was heard in camp, or on the march, that it was either 'Jackson or a rabbit.'"

Their affection for him was mirrored by the public, whose morale was obviously important to sustain the war effort. Jackson, the daring Christian soldier, was a full-fledged hero, having captured, along with a good many Yankees (it was "cheaper to feed them than to fight them," he noted), the imagination of the people. On the march into Maryland during the Sharpsburg campaign, Jackson was forced to seek shelter in a house and lock himself in a room, hoping to find peace to write a dispatch to Lee. But the crowd of women and children, not content with patting his horse or pulling hairs from its tail, began breaking the shutters of the house until Jackson gave in, opened the door, and was covered in flowers. "Really, ladies," he said with surprising savoir faire, "this is the first time I was ever surrounded by the enemy."

The magic remained after Sharpsburg, when he was accosted by a young mother who wanted him to bless her 18-month-old son. Confederate Captain Charles Blackford noted that the mounted Jackson, without hesitation or showing the slightest surprise, took the infant into his arms, "until his graying beard touched the fresh young hair of the child." The general was joined in silent prayer by his men, who removed their caps, and by the young mother, who, touching the general's mount, Little Sorrel, bowed her head. His prayer completed, Jackson returned the baby to his mother, and rode away.

Obviously, Jackson, the self-contained, uncommunicative general, whose uniform and cap were often so deeply powdered by dust that he could be mistaken for a common soldier, had command presence, whatever his eccentricities.

His leadership with his soldiers was based on an esprit de corps of men convinced that they, under his command, were the whip hand of the Confederacy; it was an esprit de corps built on the one thing that makes everything right and that won him his civilian adoration—victory. In victory, a commander's quirks and his extreme demands can add to a unit's pride, stamping that unit with the individuality that marks, as in the British army, an elite regiment.

Lee managed Jackson's genius by giving him as much autonomy as possible. The experience of the Seven Days taught Lee not to use him in intricate maneuvers that relied on Jackson's coordinating his movements with other commanders. Jackson was best riding alone, and when Lee and Jackson thought on parallel strategic tracks, as they often did, Lee felt assured that if an objective could be achieved, Jackson, under discretionary orders and with his dogged devotion to duty, would get the job done.

For all the fame Jackson earned at First Manassas (where he was given the name "Stonewall"), or in his bold Valley campaign, or for his stubborn defense at Second Manassas or at Sharpsburg, it was at Chancellorsville that Jackson's star shone most brilliantly. And it was there that he was shot down by friendly fire, mortally wounded in the twilight while scouting ahead of his lines.

As the ambulance wagon carried him along potholed roads to Guiney Station, men and their wagons coming in the opposite direction gave way, the men shouting, "I wish it were me, sir!" and offering prayers, food, and tears. An emotional General Lee, who prayed harder for Jackson's recovery than he had prayed for anything in his life, sent Jackson a message: "Could I have directed events, I should have chosen for the good of the country to have been disabled in your stead. . . . I congratulate you upon the victory [at Chancellorsville] which is due to your skill and energy." Jackson's response was to turn his face away and murmur, "General Lee is very kind, but he should give the praise to God."

When Jackson succumbed to pneumonia stemming from his wounds, the entire state of Virginia—indeed, the entire South—was plunged into mourning. Even the spartan Confederate President Jefferson Davis, who was slow to appreciate Jackson's achievements, was stunned. After Jackson's funeral, "when a friend found Davis in the [Confederate] White House staring blankly into the distance, the president bestirred himself and said: 'You must forgive me. I am still staggering from a dreadful blow. I cannot think.'"

In contemporary Virginia, Jackson is memorialized, as he would no doubt like to be, with simplicity and religion. If one drives the main interstate, I-95, one will pass a startling freeway marker. "Stonewall Jackson Shrine," it reads. *Shrine*, for such is his place in Southern hearts.

If one turns off the interstate and drives down a dusty little road, the house where Jackson died—as he wished, on the Sabbath—will come into view. There is no gift shop. There is nothing much at all, only a ranger there to talk about Jackson's final hours, to quote his poetic last words—"Let us cross over the river, and rest under the shade of the trees"—and to remind us of a hard-driving (but nonswearing) general, who fought as a tough-minded, avenging sword of Gideon, but who was also, poignantly and in the best sense, a self-made man, a loving husband, a happy children's playmate, a winsome friend, and a sincere man of God.

A. P. HILL, THE PROFESSIONAL SOLDIER

Ambrose Powell Hill was the best division commander in the Army of Northern Virginia. Like Stonewall Jackson—a man with whom he often quarreled—"Little Powell" took pride in having troops who could move fast and hit hard. He called his men "the Light Division." No one knows exactly why—most likely, it was the aesthetics of a Virginia cavalier, which A. P. Hill most assuredly was—though one trooper noted that the "name was applicable, for we often marched without coats, blankets, knapsacks, or any other burdens except our arms or haversacks, which were never heavy and sometimes empty."

If the Light Division sped to the battlefield hungry, it was not through any lack of foresight, planning, or good management on Hill's part. Hill was a professional soldier: his troops well drilled, his demands on them—and his care for them—high, their performance superb. Once, early in the war, when a commissary officer told him there was no food to be found, Hill replied: "Very well. You can report back to your company. We have no earthly use for a commissary who, in a country like this, cannot furnish regular rations for the men." Hill rode out himself, and later returned, driving a herd of beeves like a cowboy.

Like Lee, Hill was a scion of Old Virginia, his family's roots in the commonwealth going back to the 17th century, and before that to the blue blood of England. His grandfather had served under Light Horse Harry Lee, and his mother was descended from an English earl. He was, in fact, everything that a Virginia cavalier should have been—raised on horseback and country pursuits, trained in the profession of arms (at West Point, where his roommate was future Union general George McClellan), and a romantic with women (though a youthful indiscretion would cost him his health for life).

What "Little Powell" lacked in physical size—he was about five feet nine inches tall, and only about 145 pounds—he made up for in courage and drive. With fellow officers, he could be coolly formal and professional, jealously guarding his prerogatives and a stickler for protocol. But with the men, Hill could be rambunctious. As a young officer in the Mexican War, his slight build did not stop him from pushing his rough, drunken soldiers on a march, his arm "perfectly sore from beating the men into obedience [with] both fist and sword." In his early career, he would round up deserters with similar physical bravado. And in the War Between the States, he was equally happy to join his enlisted men in rough-and-tumble pursuits, chasing rabbits or squirrels, fighting bats with sticks, and hurling snowballs.

It cost him no respect, for his men saw him as "an ideal soldier," a courtly Virginia gentleman, a man who could push paperwork with "dispatch . . . [and an] urbanity of manner, so very rare, that Congress remarked upon it," a man properly set above them by birth, brains, breeding, and training, a man, as a chaplain noted, "of self-poised strength and repose . . . of great elevation of character and of broad and commanding intellect."

But he was also a man of aggressive high spirits, and for his troops, his willingness to mix it up with them was merely another sign of his physical courage and toughness, the sort of man who—in his trademark red calico "battle shirt"—could lead a charge into Hell, his men confident that they would leave the place a reeking abattoir of dead demons.

His men's confidence in him was echoed by the Confederacy's high command. Hill became the youngest Major General in the army, and he never lost the confidence of Lee or, despite their long-standing feud, of Jackson. Both Lee and Jackson, in the delirium of their deathbeds, called for A. P. Hill. Lee said: "Tell A. P. Hill he must come up!" and Jackson called on Hill to "prepare for action!" When a desperate charge had to be made, "Little Powell" would get it done.

Hill first came to prominence when Lee took command during the Seven Days campaign. It was the impetuous Hill who, at the battle of Mechanicsville, threw his men at the Federal army, beginning the Confederates' relentless offensive. Typically, Hill struck rather than wait for Jackson, whose uncharacteristic lethargy was puncturing Lee's plans. With the daylight hours for battle fading, Hill chose to attack without Jackson's support and accept the risks, rather than let opportunity—and the Yankees—slip away. It was bold, rash, costly, and perhaps foolish. But Hill never flinched from action, and Lee admired officers with an offensive spirit. Throughout the Seven Days campaign, Major General Hill and Brigadier General John Bell Hood were the two officers who most vividly and successfully executed Lee's conviction that the Federals must be driven from the outskirts of Richmond. Lee wrote of Hill that he displayed "the impetuous courage for which that officer and his troops are distinguished." If *indefatigable* was the word that defined Lee in the Mexican War, *impetuous* was the word that defined Hill in the War Between the States.

Hill was a tremendously inspiring presence in combat. He was continuously, as one observer remarked, "among the men, leading and cheering them on in his quiet and determined manner. He saw the overwhelming numbers with which they had to contend, but calmly planning his designs, he was fiery in the execution of them, giving counsel, as if in private life, but mounting his horse and dashing to the front whenever his battalions began to swerve before the masses of the enemy." At one point, during the battle at Frayser's Farm, when a brigade was breaking under fire, Hill seized the colors, rode forward and shouted, "Damn you, if you will not follow me, I'll die alone!" The men followed.

Leading from the front, by personal example, was Hill's hallmark. He used the handguard of his saber as brass knuckles to smite deserters and malingerers among his own men, rebuke teamsters who abused horses (like Lee, he had a fondness for animals), and lay into the enemy. Hill had the rare ability to be fierce and impetuous in battle, while at the same time remaining perfectly mentally composed. His ferocity did not color his thinking; he did not subordinate his mind to emotion. He had two goals always uppermost—defeating the enemy and maintaining the standard for courage in his unit. Once, as he was leading men forward into action, he passed a lieutenant among a mass of retreating soldiers. Hill tore the man's insignia from his collar, reduced him to the ranks on the spot, and warned him, "if you do not go to the front and do your duty, I'll have you shot as soon as I can spare a file of men for the purpose!" There would be no shirkers in the Light Division, at least among the officers, who had to meet Hill's level of bravery to deserve their commissions. For enlisted men, he could be more forgiving, in one instance, gently telling an emotionally shattered private to go to the rear "before you cause good men to run."

Hill, like many of his Virginian brethren, was intent on maintaining the chivalry of arms. While he would surge passionately with the blood-dimmed tide of battle, he was protective of the lives of captured officers. When in the midst of combat Union Brigadier General Henry Prince presented himself to Hill, saying, "General, the fortunes of war have thrown me into your hands," Hill replied: "Damn the fortunes of war, General! Get to the rear! You are in danger here!"

When Hill accepted the Federal surrender of Harper's Ferry during the Sharpsburg campaign, he graciously and sympathetically told Union General Julius White, "I would rather take the place twenty times than undertake to hold it once," given that Harper's Ferry rested in a pocket surrounded by high ground. Hill did not dance in the face of a vanquished foe. He was not that kind of man. He even sent commendations to Union troops whose valor against him he admired.

Hill had a gentleman's pride, and while that ensured that he treated his foes with respect, it also meant that General Lee would have a difficult time extricating Hill and Jackson from their legal wrangling against each other. Hill was in many ways Jackson's opposite. Where Jackson was a stern Calvinist, Hill was a skeptical Episcopalian who held religious enthusiasm suspect. Where Jackson kept his plans secret, even from his own officers, Hill resented Jackson's apparently arbitrary orders that brought equally arbitrary punishments if not executed slavishly. Where Jackson routinely arrested officers whose obedience he thought was qualified, Hill would not let any such action taken against him go unchallenged. Their disputes were never resolved, and Lee's attempts to achieve a reconciliation between the two West Pointers (who had disliked each other even then) never worked; so he did the next best thing. Despite Hill's remonstrances, Lee, whom Hill idolized, simply refused to do anything with the paperwork of charges and countercharges. Lee's reasoning was simple: Jackson and Longstreet were his two corps commanders, and after "these two officers, I consider General A. P. Hill the best commander with me. He fights his troops well, and takes good care of them."

If Hill fought his troops well, he also fought them hard. As Confederate officer Dorsey Pender wrote to his wife, "You have no idea what a reputation our Division has. It surpasses Jackson's Division both for fighting and discipline. . . . But when I tell you that this Division has lost 9,000 killed and wounded since we commenced the Richmond fight at Mechanicsville, you can see what our reputation has cost us."

Hill's reputation was so high that after Jackson's death, Hill became one of Lee's three corps commanders. Lee judged Hill "the best soldier of his grade with me," and later told President Davis that if officers from the Army of Northern Virginia were needed in other theaters, A. P. Hill was the one general he did not want transferred from his command.

Still, in some ways, Hill was not an obvious choice to lead a corps. First, though Hill was good at drawing up and executing military plans, he was essentially a combat soldier. He resisted having to keep his distance from the battlefield to concentrate on the broad view; and in fact, as a corps commander, he once even rushed forward to help operate an artillery piece. Second, the stress of continual campaigning had ensured that his unsteady health was now beginning a more rapid decline.

But Hill remained an aggressive fighter. At Gettysburg, he was a hawk, enthusiastically supporting Lee's plan for Pickett's charge. Even after the battle, on the retreat back to Virginia, his men displayed their general's high spirits. An observant army chaplain heard "the loud laughter of the men, comprising the head of A. P. Hill's column. . . . They fought hard . . . and were now falling back and wading to their knees in mud and mire. They were as cheerful a body of men as I ever saw; and to hear them, you would think they were going to a party of pleasure instead of retreating from a hard fought battle."

They maintained that high morale in the hard-slogging 1864 campaign against Grant. One Confederate observer recorded his astonishment at how these "lunatics were sweeping along to that appallingly unequal fight, cracking jokes, laughing, and with not the least idea in the world of anything else but victory. . . . It was the grandest moral exhibition I ever saw!" It was also a tribute to Hill's fighting spirit and to his record of successful leadership. To his men, Hill was a warrior chieftain whose wisdom, courage, and spirit could not be doubted.

One officer remembered Hill thus, at the battle of the Wilderness: "Surrounded by his staff, this beloved general, whose custom it ever was to feel in person the pulse of battle, and who always stationed himself just beyond his men in action, sat, a stately presence, anxiously awaiting the issue of events." This "beloved general," the "pulse of battle"—these were the keys to Hill's leadership. He was a "beloved general" because he looked after his men—their training, their supplies, and most of all their courage, maintaining the proud and inspiring spirit of the Light Division. Hill had the two essential qualities of instinct and courage. They drew him to the pulse of battle and guided him in responding to it.

But Hill could not overcome the debility that was creeping through his body or, for that matter, through the body of the Confederacy. A man with such an instinctive sense of the ebb and flow of battle knew that the end was drawing near, and if his country died, he wanted to die with it. In his youth, he had adopted the Latin tag *"Dulce et decorum est pro patria mori"* as his own. Now, in extremely ill health, he was ready to execute it, though it meant leaving his beloved wife and daughters behind. If Richmond fell, he confessed, he did not wish to survive.

In the early hours of April 2, 1865, the war in Virginia only a week away from its tragic culmination, A. P. Hill was desperately sick, but he continued to lead and guide his men from the front. Lee was so worried about Hill that he sent a staff officer to specifically remind him to be careful.

But Hill, the corps commander, was riding across contested ground. He captured two Federal infantrymen and sent them back to the Confederate lines under guard. He rode on with a sergeant until they saw a squad of Federal infantry, two of whom leveled muskets at Hill. Hill audaciously rode forward, pointed his cocked revolver, and commanded them to surrender. Instead, they fired, knocking Hill from his horse. By the time he hit the ground, he was dead.

A. P. Hill had served with Lee in his every major action of the war. His death, coming at the end of the war, and concomitant with the death of the civilization that made him, did not stir the same public emotion that met news of Jackson's or Stuart's death. Too much had already been lost. But he was remembered by Lee, who shed tears at the news, and could find solace only in that the gallant Hill "was now at rest, and we who are left are the ones to suffer."

The staff officer Lee had dispatched to admonish Hill to keep safe was Colonel Charles Venable. Venable later remembered Hill as "one of the knightliest Generals of that army of knightly soldiers," a leader of "those noble sons of Virginia at whose roll-call grateful memory will ever answer: 'Dead on the field of honor for the people they loved so well.'" Ambrose Powell Hill, the fighting man's general, died as he would have wished, on horseback, his revolver cocked, his "death groan," in the words of Chaplain J. Williams Jones, "lost in the roar of battle." The guns are quiet now, and in their wake, it is hard not to admire the "gallant and glorious little Powell Hill."

Requiescat in pace.

JEB STUART, THE VIRGINIA CAVALIER

The two possessions that James Ewell Brown (J.E.B. or Jeb) Stuart always carried with him were the regulations of the United States Army and the *Book of Common Prayer*. The juxtaposition of those two books was not accidental, for if anyone during the War Between the States exemplified the medieval ideals of knightly chivalry—of religion mixed with soldiering, and with a good time to be had from both—it was Jeb Stuart.

For all his knightly pretensions, Stuart did not come from a wealthy planter's family. His father was a modestly successful lawyer and politician, but Stuart had to make his own way from an early age—boarding away from home to attend school and then setting off for West Point.

Stuart consciously made himself into the very epitome of a Virginia cavalier. In the War, he was a dashing cavalryman with a plumed hat bedecked with flowers given him by flocks of admiring Southern women. He gave his camps names like *Qui Vive* and *Quien Sabe,* and surrounded himself with the Southern equivalent of a medieval court that included a minstrel (or in this case, a banjo plucker), a "fighting bishop" (the Reverend Major Dabney Ball), relations of the "King" (Robert E. Lee's son Rooney and nephew Fitzhugh), a foreign mercenary come to join the Round Table (the Prussian giant, Heros von Borcke, who after the war flew the Confederate battle flag from the ramparts of his ancestral castle), and a fierce pet raccoon for a watchdog.

It was an amazing collection of men and animals, and their effect on the enemy was electric. If Lee intimidated Northern generals with his audacity and aggressive victories, Stuart kept them in a constant state of fear that he might suddenly burst into their camps, capture them, and wreck their plans.

One of Stuart's most daring raids was on Union General John Pope's headquarters. For Stuart, it was a matter of settling a score. Pope's cavalry had ambushed him, and while he had made his escape, he had lost some of his *accoutrements,* including his famous plumed hat. Stuart's revenge came in typical Stuart fashion. Riding in search of the enemy, Stuart found a black man on horseback singing "Carry Me Back to Old Virginny." The black Virginian told Stuart he knew exactly where Pope was, and led him there.

The Union troops were bedding down. One Federal officer said to another, "I hope Jeb Stuart won't disturb us tonight." Then, as if on cue, gunfire, chaos, and the Rebel Yell burst into his ears. "There he is, by God!"

Pope, as it turned out, was not in his camp, but Stuart obtained the general's coat nevertheless, and the Union foe was thrown into confusion. During the raid, a buffalo robe remained in Federal hands only because it was guarded by a Newfoundland, and Stuart's animal-loving cavaliers would never shoot a dog—no matter how prized the booty.

Stuart was a clever man, always eager for action. Before the war, he was in Washington to obtain a patent for his invention of a saber hook when John Brown attacked Harper's Ferry. It was Stuart (in hastily acquired uniform) and his old West Point superintendent Robert E. Lee (in unostentatious civilian clothes) who planned the counterterrorist action that led to the freeing of Brown's hostages and the capture of Brown himself.

When Brown tried to defend his actions, Stuart—the teetotaling but fun-loving Episcopalian—expostulated, "But don't you believe in the Bible?" For Stuart, slavery, at a minimum, was accepted by the Bible; and in any event, its existence did not justify forcible abolition by conspiracy to commit kidnapping, armed insurrection, and murder. It is worth remembering that 19th-century moralists of so celebrated a stripe as the evangelical leader and labor reformer the Seventh Earl of Shaftesbury, and more remarkably, Samuel Wilberforce, the Anglican Bishop of Oxford (son of William Wilberforce, the best-known campaigner against the slave trade), sided with the South.

But Stuart's Southern patriotism flowed much deeper than the controversial debates over slavery. He was always a Virginia patriot. It was a matter of birth, a matter of pride, and more than anything else, a matter of identity, providing the very model, in the tradition of the Virginia cavalier, on which he based himself.

It was a tradition that rested on courage, panache, and a gentlemanly demeanor, all of which Stuart sought to instill in his cavalry. Stuart told his troops: "We *gallop* toward the enemy, and *trot* away, always." In point of fact, the "always" was an exaggeration. Stuart's war was full of swashbuckling hairsbreadth escapes, his fleeing horse bounding over fences, hedges, and gullies, his flowing moustaches once singed by a minié ball.

Though colorful, Stuart's method was not all show, bluster, and fancy. It was based on extremely hard work and brilliant insight from a comparatively young man (he was only 28 at the beginning of the war). Stuart realized from the start that his cavalry could not be used for crashing into infantry. Those tactics were outdated and led only to the slaughter of horses and their riders. He knew that his cavalry had a new role to play. It was essentially a role of reconnaissance, intelligence, and counterintelligence: reporting on Union troop movements, screening Confederate movements from the enemy, raiding Union positions for supplies, prisoners, and information (Lee praised Stuart for the accuracy of his intelligence), and, whenever possible, sabotaging and harassing enemy troops, their transport and communications.

There were three keys to Stuart's success:

First, personnel: he wanted a higher caliber of soldier; the British tradition of a gentleman buying his commission to serve in an elite regiment would have suited him perfectly (if he could have afforded it himself) because he wanted men who were brave, socially smart, and regarded fighting as a privilege. He wanted fox-hunting men: "I shall strive to inculcate in my men the spirit of the chase."

Second, planning: Stuart's dashing campaigns were carefully planned; Stuart slept little and was always active either in the field or working on his plans. For all his flash, Stuart believed that "the essential characteristic of a successful cavalry leader [is] prudent boldness." A man like Stuart who put such store on being a gay cavalier would not use the word "prudent" lightly.

Third, preparation: Stuart was diligent in training his cavalry; and believed that no training was better than live-fire action. Stuart took his green troops in front of the enemy as soon as possible, training them—as though they were horses or gun dogs—to get used to the heat and flash of enemy fire.

Stuart also believed, despite the rollicking tone of his camp, in military discipline—and enforced it. To join Stuart's cavalry, one had to be good, and he relied on the professionalism of his junior officers. Cavalry units were inevitably dispersed, and Stuart, like Lee, was good at delegating authority, which required that he have confidence in his subordinates. Stuart's "Round Table" was not just for show and merry parties. Its members were—like the knights of old—professional soldiers.

He even established a company—Q Company (later abolished)—to drain off all the slackers, malingerers, cowards, and incompetents so that they wouldn't pollute the quality of his other units. To Stuart, the men in Q Company belonged in Caliban's company—they were shameless, lazy, irresponsible, and so degradedly idiotic that they didn't know how to have fun. For Stuart, nothing was more fun than fighting and outwitting the enemy in the field. "You don't want to go back to camp," he told one of his men who was hungry. "I know. It's stupid there, and all the fun is out here. I never go to camp if I can help it."

George Eggleston, who later wrote the famous book *A Rebel's Recollections,* said of Stuart: "Indefatigable to fatigue himself, he seemed never to understand how a well man could want rest; and as for hardship, there was nothing, in his view, which a man ought to enjoy so heartily, except danger."

Stuart kept his warrior's role strictly separated from his responsibilities to his wife and family. He did not want his wife and children endangered by battle, disease, or the other hazards of war, nor did he want his responsibilities to his men and the Southern cause given short shrift because of worries for his family. He wanted his family far from the action and told his wife: "I don't care what other Generals do, all I have to say is that while this war lasts I will not leave the van of our Army unless compelled to."

The jolly cavalier was well aware of war's harsh realities. He was far removed from those foolish Northern civilians who brought picnics to watch the battle of First Manassas. He wrote at the beginning of the struggle, "I regard it as a foregone conclusion . . . that we shall ultimately whip the Yankees. We are bound to believe that anyhow; but the war is going to be a long and terrible one, first. We've only just begun it, and very few of us will see the end."

Nevertheless, he tried to enjoy his war as a merry prankster. When he seized the telegraph at Burke's Station, Stuart wired the Union quartermaster complaining that the quality of Union mules was so poor, he would have trouble transporting his loot. Most memorable of all was when Stuart took command of Lee's Second Corps at Chancellorsville after both Stonewall Jackson and A. P. Hill were wounded. Stuart rode up and down the line, gaily singing for the Federal commander, "Old Joe Hooker, won't you come out of the Wilderness, out of the Wilderness, out of the Wilderness. . . ." He also rode up to the Federal line and commanded that they cease firing on his exposed flank, which the Yankees did—

until they realized who he was, and fired volleys of lead after him.

Even when it came to rallying fleeing troops he could be witty: "Confound it, men, come back! Don't leave me alone here!"

But, as it was in Camelot, so it was for the cavalry of the Army of Northern Virginia. Their valor could not hold back the evil day. In Tennyson's words, uttered by a dying King Arthur in the *Idylls of the King:* "The old order changeth, yielding place to the new,/And God fulfils himself in many ways,/Lest one good custom should corrupt the world."

The old order that changed for Jeb Stuart was both one that he had foreseen—a rising bill of Confederate casualties—and one that he had not. The Union cavalry, which the Confederates, in their pride, thought they could always outfight and outmaneuver, was rapidly improving. The Federals had an unlimited supply of mounts and plenty of food. On the other hand, Confederate horses were in short supply, and there wasn't food enough even for the men. Time was catching up with Stuart's cavaliers.

As the campaigns grew harder, and his troopers—and the people—grew war-weary, a flaw was exposed in Stuart's leadership. His flamboyant image, which disguised the responsible officer beneath, was no longer a morale-enhancing blessing. Earlier in the war, his winning personality—and professional acumen—had made him a favorite of officers as different as Lee (who regarded him like a son), Jackson (Stuart was the one officer who could kid him without rebuke), A. P. Hill, and Longstreet (even when the latter two were feuding). But now, the voices of his detractors were rising. He was accused of being shallow, vain, immature, and self-centered; he was no longer dashing, he was reckless. War had lost its glamour, and too many had died for his critics to accept Stuart as an inspiring or admirable *beau ideal.*

One such fault-finder wrote to Jefferson Davis. "President, allow a true Southern lady to say, General Stuart's conduct since Culpepper is perfectly ridiculous, having repeated reviews for the benefit of his lady friends, he riding up and down the line thronged with those ladies, he decorated with flowers, apparently a monkey show on hand and he the monkey. In fact General Stuart is nothing more or less than one of those fops, devoting his whole time to his lady friends' company."

Many of Stuart's increasingly hard-bitten troops shared this "true Southern Lady's" view, grumbling about Stuart's misplaced priorities. They saw their job as fighting the enemy, not wearing themselves out, sometimes in wretched weather, riding in decorative parades.

Morale was slipping, and the men were exhausted. So often in this war Confederate soldiers were deprived of food and sleep, surviving on boiled coffee that could be ground-up anything. Few captured the feeling better than one of Stuart's officers, who wrote: "It is impossible for me to give you a correct idea of the fatigue and exhaustion of the men and beasts at this time. From great exertion, constant mental excitement, want of sleep and food, the men were overcome, and so tired and stupid as almost to be ignorant of what was transpiring around them. Even in line of battle, in momentary expectation of being made to charge, they would throw themselves upon their horses' necks, and even the ground, and fall asleep."

Stuart had two great maxims of war, both of which were endangered by this exhaustion: "Believe that you can whip the enemy, and you have half won the battle." And "If you are in doubt what to do, attack." Stuart's men were still proud, still hard chargers, but they recognized the growing disparity between their own ragged state and the freshly mounted, well-equipped, increasingly confident Union cavalry.

Stuart saw it too, and his response, like A. P. Hill's and Lee's, was to bring himself even closer to the battlefield. Though a corps commander with wide responsibilities for the cavalry of the Army of Northern Virginia, Stuart was not above taking command of a brigade and leading it into combat.

On May 11, 1864, Stuart fought, again from the front, at the battle of Yellow Tavern. There, he was shot by a retreating Federal's .44 caliber pistol.

"General, are you hit?"

"I'm afraid I am," he said, clutching at the blood seeping through his uniform. "But don't worry, boys. Fitz [Fitzhugh Lee] will do as well for you as I have done."

When Fitzhugh Lee himself rode up, Stuart said: "Go ahead, Fitz, old fellow. I know you'll do what is right."

When he saw retreating Confederates, Stuart shouted: "Go back! Go back! Do your duty, as I have done mine, and our country will be safe. Go back! Go back! I had rather die than be whipped."

"Well, I don't know how this will turn out," Stuart said a little later, "but if it is God's will that I shall die, I am ready."

Stuart may have been ready, but for his friends it was yet another grievous blow. Lee said of his beloved cavalryman, "I can scarcely think of him without weeping."

Later Lee would say that Stuart was his very "ideal of a soldier." For Lee, as for the writer John Esten Cooke, chivalry counted, and the perduring image was of Stuart, the happy warrior:

And *Stuart* with his sabre keen
And shooting plume appears,
Surrounded by his gallant band
Of Southern cavaliers.

JAMES LONGSTREET,
LEE'S OLD WAR HORSE

Longstreet's method of leadership was that of a sturdy professional soldier—nothing flashy, but everything done to remember that men's lives were on the line. And the men respected him for it.

Though a taciturn man, he was, at his best, an *inspiring* presence on the battlefield. As Lee's senior corps commander, Longstreet was the best administrator among his top generals. But Longstreet saw his duty as more than bringing his men to the right place at the right time. He knew he had to motivate men to face danger and win. He didn't do it through blustery words and speeches. He did it by acting as though a battle were no more dangerous for a brave man than sitting on a porch and drinking iced tea.

Cigar between his bearded lips, Longstreet was an imperturbable figure in combat. One officer in Tennessee called Longstreet "the boldest and bravest looking man I ever saw. I don't think he would dodge if a shell were to burst under his chin."

When another officer ducked as a shell passed overhead, Longstreet smiled and remarked, "I see you salute them."

"Yes, every time."

"If there is a shell or bullet over there destined for us," Longstreet replied, "it will find us."

The leader of Lee's beloved Texans, John Bell Hood, paid Longstreet the ultimate fighter's compliment when he said, "Of all men living, not excepting our incomparable Lee himself, I would rather follow James Longstreet in a forlorn hope or desperate encounter against heavy odds. He was our hardest hitter."

He was Lee's "hardest hitter" for three reasons.

First, as Lee's most reliable corps commander, he had more troops under his command than any other officer, and when he committed his men to combat, it was with carefully positioned skill, the ground surveyed, the troops at full strength. As one Virginia soldier memorably recalled: "Like a fine lady at a party, Longstreet was often late in arrival at the ball, but he always made a sensation . . . with the grand old First Corps, sweeping behind him, as his train."

Second, through his cool presence on the battlefield, he was able to transmit his own stubborn streak to his troops, making them resolute defenders and unstoppable chargers. Longstreet's greatest insight as a battlefield leader was that in every battle, somebody is bound to run, and if the troops "will only stand their ground long enough like men, the enemy will certainly run." If Lee demonstrated the military virtues of audacity, Longstreet held to the virtues of tenaciously digging in.

Third, Longstreet had a mastery of military tactics learned from experience, and calmly applied his lessons in the heat of combat. At the desperate battle of Sharpsburg, Longstreet's tactician's "eyes were everywhere." As his aide Moxley Sorrel wrote, Longstreet's "conduct on this great day of battle was magnificent. He seemed everywhere along his extended lines, and his tenacity and deep-set resolution, his inmost courage, which appeared to swell with the growing peril to the army, undoubtedly stimulated troops to great action, and held them in place despite all weakness."

The Union General Gordon Granger spoke for many frustrated Federal officers when he said, "It's no use to stop and fight Longstreet. You can't whip him. It don't make any difference, whether he has one man or a hundred thousand."

Lee called Longstreet his "old war horse," and the two generals had a cordial, respectful relationship. The British officer and observer Lt. Colonel Arthur Fremantle noted that Longstreet "is never far from General Lee, who relies very much on his judgment. By the soldiers he is invariably spoken of as 'the best fighter in the whole army.'"

The best fighter, perhaps, but certainly of Lee's early corps commanders—Stonewall Jackson, A. P. Hill, Richard Ewell, and Jeb Stuart—the only non-Virginian. Born in South Carolina, raised in Georgia, and sent to West Point by Alabama, he was easily distinguished from the Virginia gentry that dominated Lee's officers.

There was, according to one of Longstreet's aides, "a good deal of the roughness of the old soldier about him." At the end of the Seven Days campaign, for instance, one of Lee's aides presented a flask of whisky—a gift from a captured Union general. The flask was passed around. The Virginians Lee, Jackson, and Stuart abstained. President Jefferson Davis took a polite sip. But Longstreet, the campaigner, took "a good soldierly swig."

In another incident, at Sharpsburg, Longstreet called out to the equally fearless D. H. Hill, who was riding up a crest while he and Lee walked. "If you insist on riding up there and drawing the fire," Longstreet said, "give us a little interval so that we may not be in the line of fire when they open up on you." Longstreet pointed to a puff of cannon smoke and joked that Hill was its target. Unfortunately, he was right. The artillery shell plowed into the front legs of Hill's horse, severing them. Hill was stuck, unable to dismount as his rearing, screeching horse stumbled, lurched, and rolled on its bloody stumps. Longstreet had stomach enough, as a leathery old trooper, to laugh and make fun of his colleague's predicament.

In the same battle, one of Longstreet's staff officers—John Fairfax, a wealthy, fierce-eyed Virginia aristocrat never to be separated from his Bible, his portable bathtub, his supply of whisky, or his horses—blurted to Longstreet: "General, General, my horse is killed! Saltron is shot; shot right in the back!"

Longstreet gave Fairfax a "queer look," amidst this slaughter of men in the bloodiest day of the War and counseled, "Never mind, Major. You ought to be glad *you* are not shot in your own back!"

It wasn't just a lack of sentimentality about horses that separated Longstreet from the Virginians. As a leader and as a soldier, Longstreet was much more in tune with the stolid, hard-punching style of Ulysses S. Grant—his pre- and post-war close friend—than he was with the risk-taking Lee, the lightning bolt Jackson, the impetuous A. P. Hill, or the swashbuckling Jeb Stuart.

But where Grant pursued a body-blow offensive against the Confederacy, relying on the weight of Union numbers and firepower, Longstreet knew that the Confederates would have to be just as resolute, *but on the tactical defensive.*

Though Longstreet greatly admired Lee (as Lt. Colonel Fremantle noted, "It is impossible to please Longstreet more than by praising Lee"), Longstreet, as a strategist and tactician, was much more in accord with Lee's predecessor, the Virginian Joseph E. Johnston, the cautious Confederate general of would-be Fabian retreats.

Longstreet did not shy from *strategic* offensives. For example, he supported the incursion into Pennsylvania that led to Gettysburg, and was continually recommending an invasion of Kentucky in the western theater. But once an offensive was launched, he preferred to switch to the *tactical* defensive, entrenching and waiting for the enemy to attack. He was happy enough following Lee on daring campaigns—as long as he felt the army would eventually hunker down. As he exclaimed to Lee during the Maryland campaign, "General, I wish we could stand still and let the damned Yankees come to us."

Fredericksburg, where behind the stone wall at Marye's Heights his soldiers mowed down wave after wave of Union troops, was Longstreet's model battle. While Lee accepted the strength of his defensive position at Fredericksburg, he was not as tied to the tactical defensive as Longstreet was. Longstreet analyzed the South's disadvantages in manpower, money, and materiel as clearly as did Lee, Jackson, Stuart, and A. P. Hill. But Longstreet came up with a different solution from that of the Virginians. The Virginians sought audacious offensive maneuvers to shock, surprise, and crush the enemy as quickly as possible (their model battle might have been Chancellorsville), hoping to stun the Federals into thinking the cost of war was too great. Longstreet believed a more important goal was sparing the Confederacy casualties it couldn't afford by adopting the comparative safety of the tactical defensive.

Occasionally, Longstreet's caution—and his ego—caused him to stumble, as at Gettysburg, where his half-hearted execution of Lee's plans guaranteed their failure.

After Gettysburg, Longstreet was eager to try his own hand, out from under Lee's shadow, in the western theater of the war. At Chickamauga, his first engagement, he met with success, filing his troops into the right position at the right time for maximum effect. Chickamauga made him a hero in the West, where good news had been scarce. General John Breckinridge led the chorus of praise, proclaiming, "Longstreet is the man, boys, Longstreet is the man."

But Longstreet's fall was precipitate. After Chickamauga, he performed poorly at Lookout Mountain, acting oddly disengaged from his duties, and chafing at the authority of his superior officer, General Braxton Bragg. He even joined in an attempt to get Bragg removed from command.

Bragg was one of the most difficult officers in the Confederate service, and so prone to contention that he reputedly even argued with himself. But he was also a favorite of Jefferson Davis, to whom Longstreet and the other generals appealed.

Davis responded by coming to Tennessee. Gathering Bragg's generals together in Bragg's presence, he asked them, individually, to state their case against their commander. After all the generals, however reluctantly, had confessed their belief that Bragg was unfit to command, Davis reaffirmed his confidence in Bragg and returned to Richmond, leaving in his wake a commanding officer poisoned with personal animosity against every one of his subordinate generals.

Bragg, at Davis's suggestion, detached Longstreet for a quasi-independent command. His assignment was to recapture East Tennessee from the occupying Federals. If this fulfilled Longstreet's desire for autonomy, he soon wished he was back under Lee's sheltering wing. Longstreet's Knoxville campaign was a fiasco, plagued by delays, and ending in abysmal, costly failure and in ugly recriminations when he tried to pass off blame for the defeat to his former friend General Lafayette McLaws.

In a mere three months, Longstreet's star fell so drastically that he went from being "Longstreet, the man" to "Peter, the slow." One well-placed observer in Richmond, Mary Chestnut, whose husband served on Jefferson Davis's military staff, wrote: "Detached from General Lee, what a horrible failure, what a slow old humbug is Longstreet."

Even Longstreet might have been inclined to accept Mrs. Chestnut's verdict. The fact was, he was an excellent corps commander for Lee, but he was not Lee's rival, or even Jackson's, when it came to independent operations.

Worse for Longstreet's reputation in the South was what happened after the War. As a soldier, Longstreet was a cautious and clever tactician. As a politician and controversialist, he was not. The "old bull of the woods," a nickname he earned in Chickamauga, became the old bull in the china shop.

After the war, Longstreet allied himself with the Republican Party that was in charge of the Reconstruction program and won appointment to a variety of political posts. That was shock enough, but a further shock to Southern sensibilities came when Longstreet entered the battle of the books over who was to blame for the South's defeat. He had the reasonable excuse of needing to defend himself from Lee's partisans who, after Lee's death, blamed Longstreet's performance at Gettysburg for the loss of the war. But Longstreet's ill-tempered counterattack did not become a man who had enjoyed such an enduring and cordial relationship with Lee, and who had a son, born during the bitter Tennessee winter of 1863, who bore the name Robert Lee Longstreet.

Longstreet had miscalculated how he should defend his reputation. The "old bull of the woods" had simply charged a red cape. He had done the same when he became a Republican, judging that "we are a conquered people. Recognizing this fact, fairly and squarely, there is but one course left for wise men to pursue, and that is to accept the terms that are now offered by the conquerors." He did not realize that the conquering party's control would soon be replaced by the "solid" Democratic South.

Longstreet outlived most of his colleagues, and despite the controversy that surrounded him, he was an active and eager participant in Confederate veterans' activities, memorial associations, and reunions. He did not molder in retirement, but received jobs from every Republican administration, starting with his friend Grant's, until his death at age 82. He also tried his hand at farming, which he enjoyed; remarried (he was a widower), finding a bride 42 years his junior (she lived until 1962); and became a Roman Catholic (he had been confirmed, perhaps under Lee's influence, as an Episcopalian during the War).

But however many civilian jobs he held, Longstreet died like an old soldier, with his last words to his wife being, "Helen, we shall be happier in this post."

The Longstreet that deserves to be remembered is not the Longstreet of postwar squabbles.

It is the "undismayed warrior" Longstreet that staff officer Moxley Sorrel remembered as "a rock of steadiness when sometimes in battle the world seemed flying to pieces."

It is the conscience-stricken Longstreet who, after Pickett's charge, "rode back to the line of batteries, expecting an immediate counter-stroke, the shot and shell ploughed up the ground around my horse, and an involuntary appeal went up that one of them would remove me from scenes of such awful responsibility."

And most of all, it is the unmovable, unshakable Longstreet who at Appomattox disdained Union General George Armstrong Custer's demand that he surrender to General Phil Sheridan. "I am not the commander of this army," Longstreet said, glaring, "and if I were, I would not surrender it to General Sheridan."

A little later, Longstreet advised Lee, as he rode to meet Grant, "General, if he does not give us good terms, come back and let us fight it out."

Longstreet gave as much, and fought as hard, as anyone for the Southern cause. He deserves to be remembered as Lee's dependable "old war horse," always, as Douglas Southall Freeman noted, "at his best in battle," always concerned for his men, always trying to fulfill Lee's prescription of "easy fighting and heavy victories."

SELECT, CRITICAL
BIBLIOGRAPHY

Note: In the text, when quoting from original sources, I've spelled out abbreviations.

Adams, Richard. 1988. *Traveller*. New York: Knopf. Charming novel by the author of *Watership Down*, taking Traveller's view of Lee. A better book than a cynic might think.

Bedwell, Randall, ed. 1997. *May I Quote You, General Forrest?* Nashville, Tenn.: Cumberland House.

———, ed. 1997. *May I Quote You, General Lee?* Nashville, Tenn.: Cumberland House.

———, ed. 1997. *May I Quote You, General Longstreet?* Nashville, Tenn.: Cumberland House.

———, ed. 1997. *May I Quote You, Stonewall Jackson?* Nashville, Tenn.: Cumberland House.

Buchan, John. [1933] 1996. *A Prince of the Captivity*. Reprint, Edinburgh, Scotland: B & W Publishing.

Burns, James MacGregor. 1979. *Leadership*. New York: Harper Torchbooks.

Charlton, James, ed. 1990. *The Military Quotation Book*. New York: St. Martin's Press.

Churchill, Winston S. [1956–1958] 1980. *A History of the English-Speaking Peoples*. 4 vols. Reprint, New York: Bantam Books.

Clausewitz, Karl von. [1833] 1984. *On War*. Translated by J. J. Graham. Reprint, New York: Penguin Books.

Clausewitz, Karl von. [1962] 1997. *War, Politics and Power.* Translated by Edward M. Collins. Reprint, Washington, D.C.: Regnery.

Connelly, Thomas L. 1977. *The Marble Man: Robert E. Lee and His Image in American Society.* New York: Knopf.

Cooke, Alistair, ed. 1955. *The Vintage Mencken.* New York: Vintage Books. Contains H. L. Mencken's classic essay, "The Calamity of Appomattox."

Cooke, John Estem. [1867] 1997. *Wearing of the Gray.* Reprint, Baton Rouge: Louisiana State University Press.

Davis, Burke. [1956] 1998. *Gray Fox: Robert E. Lee and the Civil War.* Reprint, Short Hills, N.J.: Burford Books. A swift-moving account of Lee's war years with much to offer in highlights and pleasure.

Davis, William C. 1997. *The Illustrated History of the Civil War: The Soldiers, Weapons, and Battles of the Civil War.* Philadelphia: Courage Books.

Davis, William C., Brian C. Pohanka, and Don Troiani. 1998. *Civil War Journal: The Battles.* Nashville, Tenn.: Rutledge Hill Press.

Dowdey, Clifford. [1963] 1991. *Lee.* Reprint, Gettysburg, Pa.: Stan Clark Military Books. A neglected masterpiece.

———. [1955] 1992. *The History of the Confederacy, 1832–1865.* Reprint, New York: Barnes and Noble Books. Originally published as *The Land They Fought For,* this is one of the very best one-volume histories of the war, tremendously well written, insightful, and atmospheric.

Eggleston, George Cary. [1894] 1996. *A Rebel's Recollections.* Reprint, Baton Rouge: Louisiana State University Press. An enjoyable, nostalgic account of the Old Dominion and her heroes in the Lost Cause.

Farwell, Byron. 1992. *Stonewall: A Biography of General Thomas J. Jackson.* New York: Norton.

Flood, Charles Bracelen. [1981] 1998. *Lee: The Last Years.* Reprint, New York: Mariner Books. A beautifully achieved portrait, a classic.

Foote, Shelby. 1958–1974. *The Civil War: A Narrative.* 3 vols. New York: Random House. This is history as a fine literary art, highly recommended.

Freeman, Douglas Southall. 1935. *R. E. Lee: A Biography.* 4 vols. Reprint, New York: Scribner. The Pulitzer Prize–winning biography that is considered the standard work. But, frankly, it is not the best place to start. The journalist and historian Paul Johnson says Lee is "entombed" in this biography, and there's something to that. More accessible are Emory Thomas's biography or Clifford Dowdey's (both also cited here). Most bookshops and libraries stock the one-volume abridgment of Freeman's four volumes by Richard Harwell, also published by Scribner.

————. [1942–1944] 1970. *Lee's Lieutenants: A Study in Command.* 3 vols. Reprint, New York: Scribner. A one-volume abridgment by Stephen W. Sears appeared in 1998, also published by Scribner.

Fremantle, Arthur J. L. [1863] undated. *Three Months in the Southern States: The 1863 War Diary of an English Soldier.* Reprint, Marshall, Va.: Greenhouse Publishing. An entertaining minor gem.

Fuller, J. F. C. 1933. *Grant and Lee: A Study in Personality and Generalship.* New York: Scribner. Fuller sides with Grant.

Gallagher, Gary W., ed. 1996. *Chancellorsville: The Battle and Its Aftermath.* Chapel Hill: University of North Carolina Press.

————, ed. 1996. *Lee the Soldier.* Lincoln: Nebraska University Press. A useful compendium of contrasting views of Lee.

————. 1997. *The Confederate War.* Cambridge, Mass.: Harvard University Press.

Gordon, Lesley J. 1998. *General George E. Pickett in Life and Legend.* Chapel Hill: University of North Carolina.

Harsh, Joseph L. 1998. *Confederate Tide Rising: Robert E. Lee and the Making of Southern Strategy, 1861–1862.* Kent, Ohio: Kent State University Press.

Hart, B. H. Liddell. [1954] 1968. *Strategy.* Reprint, New York: Praeger.

Hattaway, Herman. 1997. *Shades of Blue and Gray: An Introductory Military History of the Civil War.* Columbia: University of Missouri Press.

Hayek, Friedrich von. [1944] 1994. *The Road to Serfdom.* Reprint, Chicago: University of Chicago Press. With his belief "that in the ordering of our affairs we should . . . resort as little as possible to coercion" and that "government in all its actions is [to be] bound by rules fixed and announced beforehand," Hayek's thinking is similar to Lee's.

Hayward, Steven F. 1997. *Churchill on Leadership*. Rocklin, Calif.: Prima Publishing. Certainly one of the most original and interesting books on leadership.

Horn, Stanley F., ed. 1949. *The Robert E. Lee Reader*. New York: Konecky and Konecky.

Howard, Michael. 1983. *Clausewitz*. New York: Oxford University Press. A lapidary summation of the thinking of the most important military theorist in history.

Johnson, Paul. 1997. *A History of the American People*. New York: HarperCollins.

Keegan, John. 1996. *Fields of Battle: The Wars for North America*. New York: Knopf.

Kennedy, Frances H., ed. 1990. *The Civil War Battlefield Guide*. Boston: Houghton Mifflin. A valuable survey.

Kipling, Rudyard. 1940. *Rudyard Kipling's Verse: The Definitive Edition*. New York: Doubleday.

Künstler, Mort, and James I. Robertson Jr. 1995. *Jackson and Lee: Legends in Gray*. Nashville, Tenn.: Rutledge Hill Press.

Künstler, Mort, and James M. McPherson. 1993. *Gettysburg*. Nashville, Tenn.: Rutledge Hill Press.

Lytle, Andrew Nelson. 1990. *From Eden to Babylon: The Social and Political Essays of Andrew Nelson Lytle*. Washington, D.C.: Regnery.

MacDonald, Rose Mortimer Ellzey. [1939] 1998. *Mrs. Robert E. Lee*. Reprint, Stuart's Draft, Va.: American Foundation Publications. A sympathetic portrait of Lee's wife.

Machiavelli, Niccolo. [1961] 1982. *The Prince*. Translated by George Bull. Reprint, New York: Penguin Books.

Macmillan Information Now Encyclopedia. 1993. *The Confederacy*. New York: Macmillan.

Marcus Aurelius. 1964. *Meditations*. Translated by Maxwell Staniforth. New York: Penguin Books.

McPherson, James M. 1988. *The Battle Cry of Freedom: The Civil War Era*. New York: Oxford University Press.

McWhiney, Grady, and Perry D. Jamieson. 1982. *Attack and Die: Civil War Military Tactics and the Southern Heritage*. Tuscaloosa: University of Alabama Press.

Mitchell, Joseph B. 1989. *Decisive Battles of the Civil War*. New York: Fawcett Premier. A good short history of the war.

Morison, Samuel Eliot. [1965] 1972. *The Oxford History of the American People*. 3 vols. Reprint, New York: Mentor.

Nash, George H. 1976. *The Conservative Intellectual Movement in America*. New York: Basic Books.

Newell, Clayton R. 1996. *Lee vs. McClellan: The First Campaign*. Washington, D.C.: Regnery.

Orwell, George. 1984. *The Penguin Essays of George Orwell*. New York: Penguin Books.

Phillips, Donald T. 1997. *The Founding Fathers on Leadership*. New York: Warner Books.

Robertson, James I. 1992. *General A. P. Hill: The Story of a Confederate Warrior*. New York: Vintage Civil War Library. A stirring tale, exceedingly well told by one of America's premier scholars of the war.

————. 1997. *Stonewall Jackson: The Man, the Soldier, the Legend*. New York: Macmillan. The definitive biography.

Roland, Charles P. 1995. *Reflections on Lee: A Historian's Assessment*. Mechanicsburg, Pa.: Stackpole Books.

Ropke, Wilhelm. 1960. *A Humane Economy: The Social Framework of the Free Market*. Chicago: Regnery. In 1998, the Intercollegiate Studies Institute of Wilmington, Delaware, did English-speaking readers the inestimable service of reissuing this mature, crystalline summation of what a free-market economy should aspire to achieve.

Shaara, Michael. 1993. *The Killer Angels*. New York: Random House. Pulitzer Prize–winning novel about Gettysburg. It was faithfully adapted for the big screen as *Gettysburg* (1993). The book is outstanding, the film is moving, though both take a different view of the battle than this author does.

Sifakis, Stewart. 1988. *Who Was Who in the Civil War*. New York: Facts on File. Handy reference, but short on personality.

Smith, Stuart W. 1993. *Douglas Southall Freeman on Leadership*. Shippensburg, Pa.: White Mane.

Stanlis, Peter J., ed. [1963] 1999. *The Best of Burke*. Reprint, Washington, D.C.: Regnery. An outstanding one-volume collection from the works of the towering figure of the Anglo-American political tradition that shaped Lee. Originally published as *Edmund Burke: Selected Writings and Speeches*.

Strock, James M. 1998. *Reagan on Leadership*. Rocklin, Calif.: Prima Publishing.

Tate, Allen. [1928] 1991. *Stonewall Jackson: The Good Soldier*. Reprint, Nashville, Tenn.: Sanders.

———. [1929] 1998. *Jefferson Davis: His Rise and Fall*. Reprint, Nashville, Tenn.: Sanders. Provocative, aphoristic, a must-read book to put the war in its proper world-historical perspective. Though Tate's political prescriptions are manifestly, ferociously wrong, his diagnosis is acute.

Taylor, Walter H. [1877] 1996. *Four Years with Robert E. Lee*. Reprint, Bloomington: University of Indiana Press.

Tennyson, Alfred. [1885] 1961. *Idylls of the King*. Reprint, New York: New American Library.

Thomas, Emory. 1986. *Bold Dragoon: The Life of J.E.B. Stuart*. New York: Harper and Row.

———. 1997. *Robert E. Lee: A Biography*. New York: Norton. A brilliant biography, masterfully concise and perceptive.

Vanauken, Sheldon. 1989. *The Glittering Illusion: English Sympathy for the Southern Confederacy*. Washington, D.C.: Regnery. An aesthetically pleasing and politically provocative study that deserves a wider readership.

Walzer, Michael. 1984. *Just and Unjust Wars: A Moral Argument with Historical Illustrations*. New York: Penguin Books.

Weaver, Richard M. 1989. *The Southern Tradition at Bay: A History of Postbellum Thought*. Washington, D.C.: Regnery. Essential reading for those interested in the intellectual and cultural life of the Old South.

Wert, Jeffry D. 1994. *General James Longstreet: The Confederacy's Most Controversial Soldier*. New York: Touchstone.

Wilkins, J. Steven. 1997. *Call of Duty: The Sterling Nobility of Robert E. Lee*. Nashville, Tenn.: Cumberland House. A Presbyterian pastor's view of Lee's character.

INDEX